AF688835

# THE TIMELESS INVESTMENT STRATEGY

Everything You Need to Start Making Money in the Stock Market Today

BILL GRAND

**© Copyright 2020 - All rights reserved.**

The content contained within this book may not be reproduced, duplicated or transmitted without direct written permission from the author or the publisher.

Under no circumstances will any blame or legal responsibility be held against the publisher, or author, for any damages, reparation, or monetary loss due to the information contained within this book, either directly or indirectly.

Legal Notice

This book is copyright protected. It is only for personal use. You cannot amend, distribute, sell, use, quote or paraphrase any part, or the content within this book, without the consent of the author or publisher.

Disclaimer Notice

Please note the information contained within this document is for educational and entertainment purposes only. All effort has been executed to present accurate, up to date, reliable, complete information. No warranties of any kind are declared or implied. Readers acknowledge that the author is not engaged in the rendering of legal, financial, medical or professional advice. The content within this book has been derived from various sources. Please consult a licensed professional before attempting any techniques outlined in this book.

By reading this document, the reader agrees that under no circumstances is the author responsible for any losses, direct or indirect, that are incurred as a result of the use of the information contained within this document, including, but not limited to, errors, omissions, or inaccuracies.

# Table of Contents

# Introduction: A New Investing Journey

The stock market can be your key to financial freedom.

Distel, A. (n.d.). *Turned-on MacBook Pro* [photograph]. Retrieved from https://unsplash.com/photos/DfjJMVhwH_8

Meet Jim. He's 30 years old, and has $100,000 worth of student loan debt. He's just now managed to land a job that he'd like to make a career of, but he's spent most of his 20s scraping by on minimum wage and unpaid internships. He's a hard worker, but wage stagnation has prevented him from getting any kind of meaningful raise. And the cost of living in his home city is so high that the raises he's gotten haven't made much of a difference when it comes to planning his finances. Now he finally has the funds to start thinking seriously about his retirement, but he still doesn't have much to put away every month.

Does this sound familiar? If you have anything in common with Jim, you're hardly alone. For many people, the stressors of steep bills, scant job prospects, and an unstable economy make saving for retirement seem like more of a dream than a necessity. Most people don't even start thinking about retirement until well into their 30s, and even then, they typically think about retirement in terms of "saving" or "putting away" money rather than investing it (Tweddale, 2019).

Let's return to Jim. Would it surprise you to learn that, by the time he turns 65, he will have $750,000 in his retirement account? He could do this by finding himself a really good job or landing himself a big promotion. He could win the lottery or inherit from a wealthy relative (Tweddale, 2019).

These are all ways to accrue a great deal of wealth, but Jim's strategy is easier and more reliable. All he's going to do is put $1,000 into an investment account every month from age 30 to age 40. Once there, it will continue to accrue, at a rate of seven percent, until he's 65 years old. Jim is going to save $120,000 over ten years, but that's going to turn into $750,000 through the power of compound interest (Staff, 2019).

You, too, could be like Jim. Better still, you could be like Joe, who started saving ten years earlier than Jim, at age 20. By the time Joe is 40 years old he, too, will have saved $120,000. But because he started saving earlier, he only had to put away $500 a month instead of $1,000. And because he chose to invest that money, he's going to have $1,500,000 in his retirement account by the time he's 65. The secret to financial security is not money, it's time. With this book in hand, you'll be able to use all the time you have to convert years of savings into hundreds of thousands of dollars in returns.

Investment might seem like a game or a gamble, but it only becomes that way for people who start too late. The earlier you begin investing your money, the larger your accounts become. Whether you are 19 or 45, the time to start investing your money is now. Not tomorrow, and definitely not ten years from now. Every day that goes by is a day that you are losing thousands of dollars in potential savings. Too many people find themselves struggling for financial security throughout their lives because they don't start thinking about saving their money until it's too late. Many people never invest at all, mistakenly believing that investment is only for people who have already achieved a great deal of wealth (Staff, 2019).

This book is here to make sure that you aren't one of those people. Consider this a step-by-step guide on how to invest your money in ways that are smart, secure, and guaranteed to earn you high returns. You may believe that you don't make enough money to start investing. You may believe that you're too young to start worrying about your financial future. But the truth is that investment is not only for the rich. This book will provide you with real-world examples and practical guidance to help you begin your investment journey, no matter what your current financial situation may be. Whether you have student debt, a high mortgage, or even low credit, this book will help you to create an investment strategy that works for you.

This book is organized in a chronological way, designed to walk you through the investment process step-by-step. From playing the stock market to setting up an investment account, each chapter will introduce a new phase in your investment strategy. Rather than trying to learn everything all at once, you can simply follow the book chapter by chapter, applying the concepts to your own finances.

Whether you're a complete beginner or have some experience with investments, the investment strategy outlined in this book has something you can use to improve your financial security. The strategies provided in this book are based on real-world numbers and marketplace research. New concepts and terminology are explained in clear, straightforward language designed to make you comfortable with the concepts and confident as you begin applying them to your own life.

This book, above all, is a journey. The theories and concepts introduced here will always be grounded in practical ways that you can apply them to your own finances. The goal of this book is not simply to teach you the basics of stock market trading or investment strategy. This is a fully formed investment plan; a financial GPS that will guide you through the system toward the highest possible returns. You don't have to take a course in economics or business to learn the ins-and-outs of smart investing, and you certainly don't have to have sizable savings already under your belt before you start investing your money.

The last thing you might want to do in your 20s is start planning for retirement. You're just beginning your financial life. Between rent, loan payments, and all the rest of life's expenses, it can feel like you barely have anything left to invest. You might feel just like Jim or Joe, and you may be wondering how in the world Jim ever managed to put away $1,000 a month. But remember - it's not about how much you invest, it's about how long your money is able to accrue interest.

Have you ever heard the old saying, time is money? It's more than just a metaphor. The earlier you begin investing, the less you need to invest every month in order to start making money. You don't have time to waste trying to teach yourself about dividends or 401(k) accounts, and with this book in hand, you don't have to. Follow the steps in this guide, one by one, and by this time tomorrow, you'll be well on your way to becoming a smart investor with a solid financial future.

## Free Bonus

You need to stop what you're reading right now. Hey, this sounds counterintuitive isn't it? Well, the reason is simple. I have a free bonus set up for you. The problem is this: we forget 90% of everything that we read after 7 days. Crazy fact, right? Here's the solution: I've created a printable, 1-page pdf summary for you… in regards to this book.

All you have to do now is visit billgrand.com/hello. Once you visit billgrand.com/hello, it will be intuitive. Enjoy & thank you!

# Chapter 1: Investment vs. Speculation

The Dow Jones average tends to rise over time.

Spiske, M. (n.d.). *White printed poster* [photograph]. Retrieved from https://unsplash.com/photos/5gGcn2PRrtc

The world of the stock market is approached through two main schools of thought: investment and speculation. Speculation is what most people think of when they think of "playing" the stock market. Speculators try to choose which stocks to buy and sell based on what they think the marketplace will look like in the future. But in the words of Warren Buffett, the market forecaster's only job is to make a fortune-teller look good. No one can predict the future, no matter how consistent the trends may be or how reliable the data looks. Speculation is essentially gambling, taking chances on what you think might happen, rather than looking at the reality of the marketplace in front of you.

This book is not about speculation. It's about investment. As an investor, you never "play" the market, you study it. Investors make smart decisions that are grounded in their individual financial realities and the landscape of the stock market as it *is*, not as they think it might be. Investors don't gamble, they trade. All investments are based firmly in facts. This book will never encourage you to gamble with your money, nor will it teach you how to "predict" future marketplace trends (Proctor, 2020).

As an investor, you are not going to get sidetracked by "get-rich-quick" schemes. Investors get rich slowly, which is why the more time you have to accrue your wealth, the more wealth you'll have when it's time to cash out. Investment requires patience, especially in the beginning. But the advantage you have as an investor over a speculator is security. While speculators lose their money as quickly as they earn it, the accounts of investors only get bigger. Investing guarantees you peace of mind. You can sleep soundly at night knowing that your money is safe and your future is assured. To quote Warren Buffett again, it's foolish to risk what you have and what you need for what you don't have and don't need (Proctor, 2020).

The backbone of smart, or "defensive," investing is a concept called **dollar cost averaging.** This is the process of investing the same amount of money at regular intervals of time into the same asset. The goal of this process is to protect your assets against the inevitable volatility of the marketplace. It effectively neutralizes your risk by spreading it out. Market values are constantly rising and falling, but over time, the trend is always an upward curve. Making small payments over a long period of time stops you from losing money when market values dip, while reaping the highest possible returns when the market values rise.

In recent times, this strategy is more important than ever. In today's marketplace, it's not uncommon for individual stocks to jump or plummet by as much as 10% in a single trading session. When the market is this volatile, even the most cautious and defensive investor can be tempted to make knee-jerk decisions based on momentary realities that can ultimately cost them money in the long-run. The dollar cost averaging method helps to prevent you from making those knee-jerk decisions, helping you to consistently maintain your assets even in the face of the wildest marketplace swings (Proctor, 2020).

The dollar cost averaging method asks you to treat individual assets as long-term investments. Over a certain period of time, you regularly make investments of the same dollar amount, with the expectation that the asset will slowly but steadily accrue interest over time. The investment schedule is completely up to you. Investors can choose to buy shares of that asset once per week, per month, or even per quarter, depending on what is comfortable for them in their current financial situation (Proctor, 2020).

The most important aspect of the dollar cost averaging method is its consistency. Regardless of the asset's price, you invest the exact same dollar amount every single time. It's this rigid formality that protects you from marketplace swings. When the market is down, you can buy more shares per dollar invested. When the market eventually goes back up, your dollars will buy you fewer shares, but you'll also earn that much more money on the shares that you purchased when the market was down.

Let's look at an example to illustrate how this method works. Imagine that you have $300 to invest every month. You decide to buy shares from an S&P 500 index fund on a regular monthly schedule. You've chosen this particular index fund because it's currently trading at $30 per share.

In the first month, your $300 gets you started with ten shares. If the fund increases in price to $50 the following month, then your investment will only buy you six more shares. But if the fund decreases in price to $20 per share, then you'll be able to purchase 15 shares.

Rigidly committing to investing your $300 every month, regardless of marketplace fluctuations, will greatly reduce the risk of your investment because the risk is spread out over several months. To use another example, imagine that you have $1,000 to invest in a stock that's currently trading for $100 per share. If you were to invest that money all at once, you would be able to purchase 10 shares.

But instead, imagine that you choose to invest just $250 per month over a period of four months. By the end of the fourth month, you will still have invested $1,000. In the first month, $250 will buy you 2.5 shares. But imagine that, in the second month, the price per share goes down to $90. In the second month, $250 will buy you 2.78 shares. In the third month, the price goes down to $85, which gets you to 2.94 shares. And finally, the price goes down to $80 in the fourth month, which buys you 3.12 shares (Proctor, 2020).

At the end of four months, you will have 11.34 shares instead of the 10 that you would have if you invested your $1,000 all at once. An extra 1.34 shares may not seem like much, but 1.34 shares worth of extra profit for every dollar of stock price growth in the future. And since you'll continue to buy shares even when the market is down, your account never decreases in value (Proctor, 2020).

In addition to risk-reduction, the second biggest advantage of dollar cost averaging is that it removes emotion from the investment process. In personal relationships, remaining connected to your feelings is healthy and beneficial. But in the world of investment, emotional decisions can cost you a great deal of money. In the face of huge marketplace swings, it can be extremely tempting to try to "time" the market. It will be tempting to increase your investments when prices are cheap, hoping to make a huge profit when the market swings up again. But this kind of erratic behavior increases your risk. This is how even smart investors end up losing money. If you rigidly make the exact payments every single time, you won't be allowing your own fears and excitements to control your financial future.

It can't be stated enough - the stock market is impossible to predict. Just because a stock or fund dropped by 30% this week does not mean that it's going to rebound by 20% next week, or even next month, for that matter. Constantly hopping in and out of stock positions is guesswork. Predicting marketplace trends is extraordinarily difficult even for investment professionals who spend 40+ hours a week studying the market. You almost certainly have better things to do with your time and your money. If you make yourself an investment schedule and stick to it, then you'll never have to worry about marketplace trends again. While other investors are up all night watching the market rise and fall, you'll be sleeping soundly with the knowledge that your assets are secure.

Dollar cost averaging stops you from becoming emotionally invested in marketplace fluctuations. You won't feel the need to panic when the market falls, nor will you be tempted to risk your hard-earned money on high-risk investments. Dollar cost averaging keeps you secure, but it also keeps you smart when deciding which asset to purchase in the first place.

Unfortunately, no investment method is fool-proof. Dollar cost averaging does have a few drawbacks. First and foremost, the marketplace tends to go up more than it goes down. This means that it can take a while before you start making any real profits on your investments. To illustrate how this works, let's return to our previous example. You have $1,000 to invest, and you've chosen to invest in an asset that's currently trading at $100 per share. Rather than investing your $1,000 all at once, you decide to spread it out over four months at $250 per month. In the first month, your $250 earns you 2.5 shares. But imagine that in month two the price per share increases to $110. Now your $250 will only buy you 2.27 shares. In the third month, the price increases to $115, which only earns you 2.17 shares. And in the fourth month, the price climbs to $120, which only gets you 2.08 shares (Proctor, 2020).

At the end of the four months, you'll only end up with 9.04 shares, rather than the 10 shares you would have earned if you had invested your $1,000 all at once. So while dollar cost averaging will protect you when the market is low, it can hold you back when the market is high. And long-term S&P 500 data does indicate that high, or "bull" markets, tend to last longer than low, or "bear," markets. Investing your money all at once is called "lump-sum" investing, and many investors choose this method over dollar cost averaging because they don't want to wait for the market to go through a cycle of falling and rising before they start making money on their investments (Proctor, 2020).

At the end of the day, the investment method that you choose is up to you. But if you're like most 20- or 30-somethings, then you probably don't have a big chunk of money to invest in a lump-sum scheme. The dollar cost averaging method helps you to budget a set amount of money every month that you'll put toward investment assets. It's a slow-and-steady method, but the more time you have, the more money you will make in the long-run. In real life, your investment schedule won't be a mere four months. You'll be choosing an investment schedule that you plan to stick with for the next ten *years*. No matter how long it takes your asset to start earning you money, when you do start earning, your profits will climb exponentially. You have time on your side, and that means you don't have to start making a profit tomorrow. You're playing the long-game, and that means you can afford to wait for your wealth to accumulate.

## Speculation and the Flawed Theory Behind It

Research the company or companies you want to invest in.

Chong, N. (n.d.). *flat black screen computer monitor* [photograph]. Retrieved from https://unsplash.com/photos/N__BnvQ_w18

In many ways, speculation is the opposite of investing. Speculators study the market as it rises and falls, hoping to cash in on sudden swings. Speculators trade assets, rapidly buying and selling assets in an attempt to profit from potential upswings. If you have a great deal of money to play with, then there's nothing inherently wrong with a speculative approach to the stock market. But most of us don't have hundreds of thousands of dollars to lose on a high-risk investment, especially when we're young. Speculation is like a hobby or even a career, something that people devote themselves to full-time in an attempt to make a huge profit in one lucky move. While it's true that you might strike it rich, you could just as easily lose your entire life savings. Investment is a long-term plan, done with the intention of increasing your financial security. Speculation, on the other hand, might make you more money, but it always decreases your security, because you never know if your investments will bring you wealth or ruin (Yeo, 2017).

Investors make their decisions based on the asset itself. They buy now with the intention of making that money back, with interest, in the future. And investment doesn't only apply to stocks. Whether you're choosing to sink your money into apartments, farms, commodities, or the stock market, an investor always looks at the asset as a money-maker in the distant future (Yeo, 2017).

For this reason, the initial price or value of the asset is not important to an investor. An investor's primary concern is making money in the future. When choosing an asset, investors aren't thinking about what will make them money the quickest, they're thinking about what will make them the most money in the long-run.

Investors are always thinking in the long-term, and therefore understand the difference between "price" and "value." Price is what you pay for something, but value is what you get from it. In the world of investing, the ultimate value should always be more than the initial payment price. This is why dollar cost averaging is such a popular method for young investors. They are not concerned about what the market is going to look like tomorrow or next week. They understand that, over the course of years, any business is going to continue to make money. The overall trend will always be upward, and that means that, as long as the investor sticks to their chosen investment schedule, they will end up earning far more than they paid for their investments.

Speculators, on the other hand, are more concerned with the price of the asset than with the asset itself. Speculators look for the cheapest assets that are predicted to increase in value over the next quarter. They buy up as much as they can while the asset is cheap, hoping to turn over a huge profit within a very short time.

To many, speculation sounds like gambling, especially if you accept the reality that marketplace trends are unpredictable. But the difference between speculating and gambling is that gamblers don't need to be part of the system into which they're sinking their money. For example, imagine you cast a bet on the outcome of a football game. The football game's operation and ultimate outcome exist independently of your bet. If you bet nothing at all, the game will go on with the same outcome. If you bet thousands of dollars or just a few, it doesn't matter. Gambling is 100% based on luck, and the gambler always exists independently of the system off which it's making money (Yeo, 2017).

Speculators, on the other hand, are still part of the system. They are active "investors" in the economic system, and the amount of money that they choose to invest can have an impact on the failure or success of the asset they're trying to profit from. Speculators don't blindly place bets and watch the market change from afar. They buy up cheap assets that they have reason to believe will quickly increase in value and make them a handsome profit in a short amount of time (Yeo, 2017).

The major flaw in the theory of speculation is assuming that marketplace predictions are possible. The marketplace doesn't exist in a vacuum, and trends don't rise and fall based on a closed, internal system. Marketplace trends are affected by political events, social upheaval, and even public opinion. A speculator in December 2019 would have no idea that the coronavirus pandemic would take the world economy by storm just one month later. When CEOs fall out of popular favor, shares in their companies can decrease. And individual businesses are constantly working to turn a profit. A business that seems like it's struggling now may turn itself around in five or ten years. A speculator will miss out on those earnings, but an investor will weather the storm. And on the flip side, a speculator may invest a great deal of money in anticipation of an upcoming advertising campaign or political election, only to find that the public response to those events was very different from what was expected.

Speculators don't look at the asset itself, they just look at the asset's price action. But looking at the marketplace numbers as simple numbers is misleading. An investor understands that share prices and marketplace trends are reflections of events happening in real life. Those numbers are based on business deals, international relations, major political events, and even public opinion of certain assets. Investors understand that prices are constantly changing, and so they don't invest for price, they invest for value. Investors choose assets that they can reasonably expect will still be making money in ten or even twenty years from now. Speculators believe that tomorrow is easier to predict than ten years into the future, but in the world of finances, the truth is quite the opposite.

If you're looking for a secure investment strategy, you're not counting on your investments to pay your bills. The money that you're putting in now you aren't expecting to get back for a long time. This is the wealth that you will retire on, the wealth that will help you to live in security and comfort *after* a lifetime of working and budgeting like everyone else. Dollar cost averaging helps to make investment possible for people of all incomes because it allows the individual to invest only what they have to spare. If you choose to invest $5 a week in your chosen asset because that's all you have after you've paid your bills, that's ok. If you have $500 a month to invest, that's ok too. No matter how much you put in, you will get back more. But in order for you to turn a profit, you have to wait. Like tending a vegetable garden, investors maintain their assets and watch their profits grow, understanding that they won't be able to reap the fruits of their labor for a long time (Yeo, 2017).

Speculators, on the other hand, often don't have an income. They don't have another way to pay their bills or maintain their lives. Speculation is a career unto itself, because in order to have any hope of turning a profit they have to study the marketplace in real-time. They have to know as much as they can in order to make accurate predictions, and even then, they often find themselves losing just as much as they gain. Speculation isn't a long-term plan for security, it's an attempt to make a lot of money in a short amount of time.

How long that money lasts depends on the speculator, the asset, and the whims of a highly volatile marketplace (Yeo, 2017).

For this reason, speculators take on a lot more risk than investors do. There is no such thing as a zero-risk investment, and even the most defensive and careful investors sometimes lose money. But speculators understand that there's a chance of losing the entire principal investment amount, which is nearly impossible for a defensive investor. You may lose something on an investment, but you'll rarely lose everything. Speculators, on the other hand, lose everything - all the time.

While you'll find speculators and investors in multiple different economic arenas, there are certain territories that are more likely to attract investors than speculators, and vice versa. Investors typically stick to the stock market, bonds, U.S. treasuries, mutual funds, and property. These are all investment markets that, slowly but surely, trend upward. In spite of wide fluctuations, these markets are relatively stable in the long term. These are markets where, if you invest your money in a regular and disciplined way, you are almost guaranteed to find yourself with huge profits in ten or twenty years' time.

Though plenty of speculators do "play" the stock market, speculators tend to be drawn to markets that are less stable, where lots of money can be made (or lost) in a very short amount of time. These kinds of markets are places like options, futures, foreign currencies, startup companies, and cryptocurrencies. These markets are either too new or too volatile to be viable places for investment. The risk involved in any of these markets is extremely high, but speculators are drawn to them because the potential profits to be made are also extremely high (Yeo, 2017).

The difference in goal planning is referred to as the investment's "time horizon." The time horizon is very long, often decades into the future. The time horizon for speculators, on the other hand, is quite short, often less than a year. And the time horizon for gamblers is shortest of all. Gamblers are expecting to win or lose money within the same day, and are rarely doing anything in the way of planning or strategizing for the future (Yeo, 2017).

The level of risk is the key difference between the financial styles. Investors have only a moderate risk. There are no guarantees, but the longer the investment schedule, the more stable the investment is, and the lower your risk becomes. Speculators, on the other hand, have a very high risk. They could make a significant profit, but they could also lose everything, and spend a lifetime trying to make back the money that they earned. And gamblers have the highest risk of all. Gambling money is made and lost so quickly, and in such arbitrary ways, that it's nearly impossible to devise a gambling "strategy."

Gamblers are literally betting their security on forces beyond their control. Whether or not they make a profit is left almost entirely up to chance.

## Introducing Mr. Market and the Market Psychology

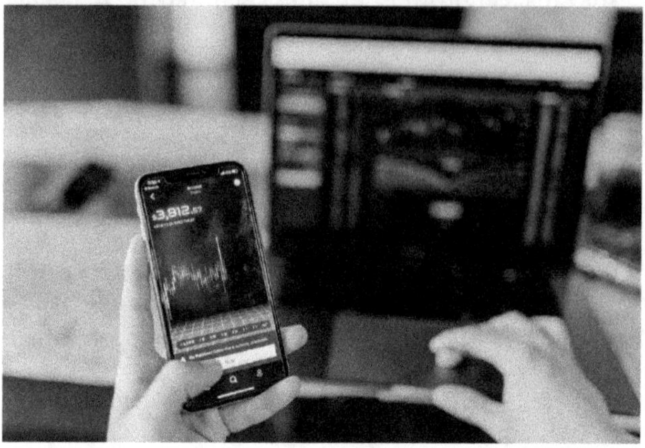

Investing in the market, without involving your emotions, is key.

Distel, A. (n.d.-a). *Person using phone and laptop computer* [photograph]. Retrieved from https://unsplash.com/photos/EMPZ7yRZoGw

To help people better understand the financial marketplace, investor Benjamin Graham published an investment guide in 1949 called *The Intelligent Investor.* In this book, he introduced a character called Mr. Market, which he used as an allegorical tool to represent marketplace fluctuations, and guide investors as to the best way to handle those fluctuations.

In his book, Graham asks the reader to imagine that they are the owner of a business. Their partner and co-owner is a man named Mr. Market. This partner is frequently offering to sell his share of the business to the reader, but just as often makes offers to the reader to buy their share. In the allegory, this partner is characterized as having a manic-depressive personality, with mood swings that range from wildly optimistic to toxically pessimistic. The reader is always free to decline Mr. Market's current offer, as they know that his mood will soon change and a new offer will soon be on the table (Wikipedia Contributors, 2020).

Mr. Market is said to be manic-depressive, or what we would today call bipolar. He is emotional, euphoric, and moody, swinging between extremely high highs and equally low lows. He is often irrational, allowing his mood to dictate his business dealings more than any logical guidance or considerations. The transactions that he offers are strictly at your option, meaning that you are free to accept or decline at your convenience, secure in the knowledge that he'll soon be back with another offer depending on where his moods take him. He is there to serve you, but he is not there to guide you. He has nothing to offer you in the way of advice, and even if he *could* advise you, his moods are so unpredictable that you would be unwise to trust anything that he had to say (Wikipedia Contributors, 2020).

Graham describes him as being a voting machine in the short term, but a weighing machine in the long term. In other words, his short-term decisions are based more on current trends, sociopolitical moods, and popularity than anything financially concrete. On the other hand, his long-term decisions are based more in values and numbers, and though his moods might seem erratic from day to day, they reveal certain patterns when looked at over the course of years. He will sometimes make you savvy business offers, but he will just as frequently give you the option to buy low or sell high. Despite all this unpredictability, you keep him on as a business partner because he is frequently efficient - but not always. At the end of the day, it's your financial savvy that's keeping the business afloat (Wikipedia Contributors, 2020).

Mr. Market's mood swings are erratic in the sense that you have no idea when he'll be feeling up or down. However, they do have a certain predictability, in the sense that you can expect frequent changes. Therefore, you can always wait to buy until Mr. Market is in a low mood and offers you a low sale price. You have the option to buy at that low price, or wait for his next low mood to see if you can get an even better offer. To this end, Graham stresses that patience is the most important quality the reader can have when doing business with Mr. Market.

Mr. Market has proved such a useful allegory for explaining investment psychology that it remains a popular teaching tool to this day, about 70 years after Graham published his book. The allegory makes it extremely clear that the only reason for the changes in Mr. Market's price offerings are his emotions. A rational person, or an intelligent investor, will wait until the price is high before he sells, and wait for the price to fall before he buys. The intelligent investor, however, will not sell *because* the price is high, nor will they buy *because* the price is low. There is no need to capitalize on the current situation because you know that same situation will come around again and again. All you need is patience. The ultimate financial decisions should be up to the investor. If you decide you want to sell, you wait for prices to climb. If you decide you want to buy, you wait for the prices to drop. The intelligent investor won't let the whims of the marketplace influence their financial decisions. Instead, they will wait patiently for the marketplace to offer the right circumstances for them to fulfill their own financial goals (Wikipedia Contributors, 2020).

To determine whether or not you want to continue investing in an asset, or sell with the intention of cashing you, Graham advises determining whether the stock valuation of a company is reasonable after the investor calculates its value via fundamental analysis. This might sound complicated, but it's actually a fairly simple process. Fundamental analysis simply means looking at a business from a big-picture perspective. You don't just look at the value of the business's current assets, you also look at its liabilities, earnings, health, competitors, and the state of the market. You consider the company's worth in the greater context of the economy it belongs to. This will help you determine whether or not it's a worthwhile investment for you. This is how you determine whether or not a company will continue to make you money as an investor twenty years into the future (Wikipedia Contributors, 2020).

Warren Buffett frequently quotes from Graham's book, and is one of the primary figures responsible for making the Mr. Market analogy a common tool used by investors to this day. It's a very simple way to express a concept that can be difficult for first-time investors to understand - there is often no rational explanation for why stock market prices rise and fall. There are so many factors at play that contribute to the market's fluctuations that trying to understand them is pointless. It's like… well, it's like working with someone who is severely manic-depressive. Their mood swings are motivated by internal chemistry and personal triggers. They may not always follow any kind of logical or predictable pattern. As such, trying to let market trends guide or influence your investment decisions is like allowing an emotionally unstable person to run your business.

The parable of Mr. Market helped Graham to introduce a market concept he called the "margin of safety." The margin of safety is how much risk is involved in a potential investment. The higher the margin of safety, the lower the risk. The lower the margin of safety, the higher the risk. Mr. Market's mood swings might make an offer seem attractive at the moment, but you, as his partner, must be able to see beyond the price he puts on the table. You have to take a look at what he's actually offering. If the price is right but the offer is risky, then the margin of safety is too low for it to be a good investment. If, on the other hand, Mr. Market makes a sound offer for too high of a price, then your job is to look ahead into the future. How much value do you stand to make from purchasing now? Can you afford to wait for another change in Mr. Market's moods, to see if you can get a lower price for the same offer?

Remember, there is a big difference between price and value. Benjamin Graham used his Mr. Market analogy to found an entire theory of investing called "value investing." Value investing means waiting to buy stocks or otherwise invest in assets when the stock is worth more than its price on the market. Don't choose assets based on how they're priced. Choose assets based on their *potential* price. To this end, Graham advised reading the financial statements and footnotes of unpopular or neglected companies with low market values. Do these companies have any hidden assets, including investments in other companies, that the market at large may be neglecting at this moment? What is the potential for growth that these companies have? Do you see this company making money ten years into the future? What about twenty? Just because the company is undervalued now means nothing. Eventually, the market will see what you see, and when the market prices go up, you'll start seeing huge returns on your initial investments (Wikipedia Contributors, 2020).

This mentality is the secret to good, defensive investing. The more you start to view the stock market through the personality of Mr. Market, the less emotionally susceptible you will be to its constant and erratic changes. Rather than obsessively watching the stock market reports every day, you'll be able to maintain a cool, emotional distance when making your investment schedules and choosing the best asset in which to invest your money. The Mr. Market analogy has been helping investors for decades to protect themselves from "emotional bias." This is what happens when our emotions initiate a shift in our perceptions, causing us to view situations in a way that affects our decisions making.

Emotional bias can cause us to look at neutral events from a negative perspective, or to believe that something is positive even when there is objective evidence to the contrary. Emotional bias can make it very difficult for us to accept hard facts, especially when those facts are unpleasant or give evidence to a reality that we don't want to accept. Emotional bias causes us to behave like Mr. Market. It causes us to make risky decisions out of excitement, and miss solid investment opportunities out of fear. When we make too much of the market's senseless fluctuations, we allow our dreams, hopes, and fears to interfere with our ability to make sound financial decisions (Wikipedia Contributors, 2020).

Intelligent investors don't need to keep on top of market trends because they understand that that's all they are - trends. Lows will become highs, which will become lows again. The only winning game in the investment world is the long-game. The more time you can sink into an asset, the more money you will make, regardless of the size of your investments. The trick, however, is to dedicate that time to an asset that is stable, reliable, and low-risk.

# Chapter 2: Push the Snowball off the Hill

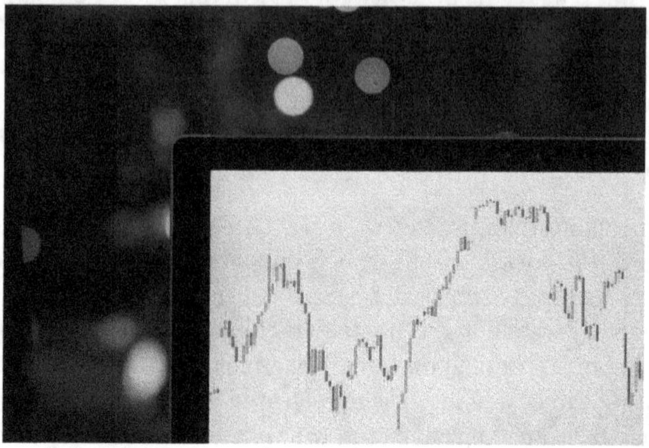

Daily, weekly and even monthly or yearly changes don't matter much when you're investing for the long-term.

M, M. (n.d.). *selective focus photography of graph* [photograph]. Retrieved from https://unsplash.com/photos/ZzOa5G8hSPI

The ultimate goal of investing your money is to earn back more than your initial investment. This is what makes it different from simply saving your money. Invested money doesn't just wait for you - it grows. The longer it sits in savings, the bigger it grows, which is why time is the key ingredient to a profitable investment strategy. But why does invested money grow? How can it be that money simply sitting in an account can earn you profit?

The secret is called compound interest (Robbins Research International, Inc., 2020).

The number one reason that investors fail to make big returns on their investment is because they don't fully understand this simple concept. Compound interest is the reason that the amount you invest doesn't matter. Too many people make the mistake of thinking that investing is something that you do *after* you already have a sizable savings. But the ultimate goal of investing is to grow your savings. Even the smallest investment can swell into hundreds of thousands of dollars given enough time. A small investment that spends years accruing interest will always result in a higher profit than a large investment that doesn't have as much time to grow. It's accrued interest that makes investments profitable, not the investment itself (Robbins Research International, Inc., 2020).

Think of your investment like a snowball rolling down a hill. The size of the snowball when it reaches the bottom has nothing to do with how big a ball you started with - it's about how high the hill is. Sure, if you build a big snowball and roll it down the hill, it will be bigger at the bottom. But your hill is short, it's not going to grow very much. On the flip side, a tiny snowball rolling down a very big hill is going to pick up a great deal of snow. At the base of the big hill, you'll end up with quite a big snowball indeed.

In this example, the snowball is your investment, the hill is the amount of time you have, and the snow is the compound interest. Perhaps another way to think about it is planting a tree. The size of the seed has nothing to do with how big or fast your tree grows. Even the tiniest seed can grow into a massive tree if it gets the right amount of sun, water, and is planted in healthy soil. To tap into the power of compound interest, you have to stop thinking about your investments in terms of money, and start thinking about them in terms of time. No matter how old you are, the best time to start investing was 10 years ago. The second best time to start investing is right now.

So what exactly *is* compound interest? Albert Einstein called it the most important invention in all of human history, but that hardly helps us to understand how it works in real, financial terms. If you don't understand compound interest now, don't worry. Many people have never even heard of it, and that's why so few people take advantage of it (Robbins Research International, Inc., 2020). But you are no longer going to be one of those people.

We'll begin with the dictionary definition of compound interest, which reads "a method used to calculate interest paid on both the principal and on accrued interest." To put this more simply, compound interest is interest paid on interest. Rather than taking the initial interest on your investment as a payout, you reinvest it. When the next period comes around, the interest that you've earned is not only on the principal sum, but on any interest that was previously accrued on that sum. The actual amount of money you'll earn in compound interest will depend on how much money you've invested, the percentage of interest paid on that amount, and the number of times per year that interest is paid out. Depending on the account, interest could be paid out yearly, half-yearly, quarterly, monthly, weekly, daily, or even continuously. The rate at which interest is paid on your account is called the "compounding frequency." The more frequently interest is compounded on your investment, the more money you will make (Robbins Research International, Inc., 2020).

To demonstrate how this works, imagine that you open an investment account and invest $100. If the annual compound interest rate is 3%, then by the end of the first year, that $100 will have grown to $103. But the following year, you won't just earn interest on that initial $100 - you'll be earning interest on $103, which means that your account will earn $3.09 in interest instead of $3.00. So the year after that, you'd be earning interest on $106.09, so on and so forth. After 20 years at this rate, your initial $100 will have grown to $180.61.

Simple interest, on the other hand, is interest that's only paid on the principal sum. So in the previous example, if you had a simple interest rate of 3% rather than a compound interest rate, you would only earn $3.00 in interest every year, no matter how much money you had accrued in interest. After 20 years on a simple interest rate, your account would only have grown to $160. With compound interest, the exact same amount of money at the exact same interest rate would make you $20 more. And while that may not seem like much, if you have 30, 40, or 50 years to let your money sit and accrue interest, compound interest could potentially make you $40, $60, or even $80 more than simple interest.

Another important concept is the difference between APR and APY. APR, or annual percentage rate, is the annual rate of interest that *doesn't* factor in compounding. APY, or annual percentage yield, on the other hand, is the annual percentage rate that reflects the entire amount of interest paid on the account, including interest that's been compounded. Both of these numbers reflect the amount of interest paid on a 365-day period (Robbins Research International, Inc., 2020).

When considering an account in which to invest, you can use a simple formula to calculate how much money you'll earn annually off the initial investment. The compound interest formula is A=P(1+r/n)(^nt). This might look complicated, but it's actually quite straightforward.

The "P" in the formula stands for the principal amount, or the initial sum of money that you've invested into the account. "R" is the interest rate, and should be entered into the formula as a decimal amount. So if the interest rate is 3%, you should enter it into the formula as 0.03. "N" is the number of times interest is compounded in a single year. So if interest is compounded yearly, N would be entered into the formula as 1. The "t" in "nt" is the amount of time that the money is invested for. So if you plan to let your investment sit for 20 years, and interest is compounded annually, then nt would be entered into the formula as 1(20). Remember that "nt" is an exponent. So if the interest is compounded once a year for 20 years, you will take the number inside the first set of parentheses and raise it to the 20th power, and multiply that number by P (Robbins Research International, Inc., 2020).

Let's look at an example to get a good idea of how the formula works. Imagine that you want to invest $5,000 into an account with an interest rate of 5% that is compounded monthly. Your formula would look like this: A=5,000(1+0.05/12)(^12(10)). First, calculate 0.05/12. Then add 1. Raise that number to the 120th power, since "nt" in this equation is 12 x 10, or 120.

Multiply that number by 5,000. If you do the math, you'll see that the final results are $8,235.05. So in 10 years' time, your initial investment of $5,000 will have grown to $8,235.05. But if you contribute an additional $5,000 to your account every 10 years, then after 20 years your account will have grown to $21,798.25.

Let's look at a few more examples to really understand how compound interest can be used to make you as much money as possible on your investments.

### Example One

You have $10,000 to invest for a period of five years. The account you choose has a 3% interest rate that is compounded monthly. At the end of five years, your initial investment will have grown to $11,616.17. If you contribute an additional $10,000 to your account every five years, then after 10 years your account will have grown to $25,109.71 (Robbins Research International, Inc., 2020).

### Example Two

You have $10,000 to invest for a period of two years. The account you choose has a 2% interest rate that is compounded quarterly. At the end of two years, your initial investment has grown to $10,404.07. If you contribute an additional $10,000 to your account every two years, then after four years your account will have grown to $21,234.66 (Robbins Research International, Inc., 2020).

### Example Three

You have $1,000 to invest for one year. The account you choose has a 5% interest rate that is compounded twice a year. At the end of the year, your initial investment has grown to $1,050.63. If you contribute an additional $1,000 to your account every year, then after two years your account will have grown to $2,154.44.

As you can see, compound interest means that the money you invest grows exponentially every time interest on the account is compounded. So if you stick to a regular investment schedule, then every time you raise the principal on the account, you start earning back double and triple the amount that you're investing.

This is why time is on your side when it comes to compound interest. The longer you invest, the higher the principal in your account becomes. Soon, you don't have to invest anything to begin earning back hundreds of times in interest what you initially invested.

To understand this concept better, let's take a look at two best friends. Their names are Ellen and Chandra. When these two women are 20 years old, Chandra decides to open an investment account. Every year, over a period of 20 years, she invests $4,000 at a growth rate of 10% per year. At age 40, she stops contributing her yearly $4,000, but lets her account continue to accrue interest every year until she turns 65 years old. When she finally decides to withdraw, she will have almost $3 million in her investment account.

Now let's take a look at Ellen. She doesn't decide to open an investment account until age 40. Her plan is identical to Chandra's. Her plan is to invest $4,000 every year until she turns 65 years old. She will actually be contributing more money to her account, saving over a period of 25 years. That's five more years (or $20,000) than Chandra. Her growth rate is also 10% annually, the same as Chandra's. But at age 65, when she goes to withdraw, she will barely have $500,000 in her account. That's 600% less profit than Chandra (Robbins Research International, Inc., 2020)!

Chandra actually contributed less money, and saved for less time. But because she had an additional 25 years to let her savings grow, she made substantially more money than her friend who started saving later in life. Compound interest means gathering interest on top of interest. So the longer you can let your savings accrue, the more money you stand to make, no matter how small your regular investments are (Robbins Research International, Inc., 2020).

No matter how old (or young) you are, the time to start investing is now. Don't wait for that big bonus or raise to open an investment account. You may not think you have enough money to spare toward a regular investment schedule, but people of *all* incomes have the ability to invest.

If you're still skeptical, meet William. He's 20 years old. He still has two more years of college left to go, but he's already accrued $60,000 worth of student debt. He's working part-time at a minimum wage job to pay his rent while he's in school. He has no savings, no assets, and until he starts paying back his student loans, no credit. But he's going to the back to open an investment account. His investment schedule? $1 a week.

That's right, $1 a week. That's $4 a month. At an APY of 0.25%, his savings will grow to $527 after 10 years. It will grow to $1,067 after 20. After 20 years, he can choose to increase his contributions, or he can stop, and let that $1,067 continue to accrue interest for another 25 years until he retires. If he increases his weekly contribution to just $10, at the same interest rate, he'll have $5,266.60 in savings after 10 years, and $10,665 after 20 years, which he can then let sit and accrue interest for an additional 25 years before he retires.

Compound interest basically supercharges your savings account. The more you have in savings, the more interest you accrue. The more interest you accrue, the more interest you accrue on that interest. Though it starts slow, especially if you don't have much to contribute in the beginning, it doesn't take long for your profits to start doubling and tripling every year.

Even a basic savings account at your personal bank can be set up with compound interest. This investment account is by far the least risky. However, most U.S. accounts have extremely low APYs. Like William, the interest rate on a basic savings account is most likely to be well under 1%. This is why defensive investors tend to put their money into investment accounts that will earn them a bit more money. Account types such as Roth IRA, SEP IRA, 401(k), or Coverdell ESA are all very low-risk, secure places to invest your money where it's fairly easy to find APYs at 1 or 2%, if not more.

Most of these accounts are retirement accounts, and are set up with the understanding that you are not going to be withdrawing your money until you reach retirement age. Coverdell ESA accounts are education accounts that parents can open when their children are born and regularly contribute to until their child is ready to go to college, at which point they can withdraw their savings and all the compound interest they've accrued over the years (Robbins Research International, Inc., 2020).

So even if you only have $1 a week or $5 a month to spare, now is the time to start investing your money. Slowly but surely, that $5 will start to grow into something much bigger. And if you get a better job or a raise, maybe you can turn that $5 a month into $5 a week, which will exponentially increase your earnings thanks to the compound interest that you accrue with each investment (Robbins Research International, Inc., 2020).

## The Rule of 72

Don't over-complicate investing - keep it simple, and timeless.

Nowakowski, A. (n.d.). *Man sitting in front of the laptop* [photograph]. Retrieved from https://unsplash.com/photos/MFms-wkv3Ow

The beauty of compound interest is that it's essentially free money. It's money that you earn without having to do a thing. But as you've already experienced, determining how much money you stand to make based on principal, regular contributions, and interest rate can require a great deal of math.

If your head is spinning from all the numbers, letters, and formulas, don't worry. The website moneychimp.com has a handy compound interest calculator that helps investors to determine how much they stand to earn in compound interest from current or potential accounts.

The calculator will ask you for the amount of the current principal, as well as the amount of future additions, which will save you from manually calculating the compound interest formula for every single additional investment. The compound interest calculator will also ask you how many years you plan to make these additional investments, your current interest rate, and how many times interest is compounded on the account annually. You can use the calculator to determine both how much money you stand to make while you're saving, and find out how much the account will grow once you've invested your planned amount (moneychimp.com, 2020).

Let's look at a few examples. Imagine that you're considering opening an investment account. The APY for the account is 20%. You would like to make an annual investment of $1,000 into the account over the course of the next 20 years, bringing your overall investment to $20,000. To start out, your principal amount is only $1,000. The annual addition to the account will also be $1,000, as that's the total amount of your annual investments. Years to grow will be 20, as that's how many years you plan to invest $1,000/year into the account. The APY is 20%, so you can enter that into the calculator as a 20% interest rate compounded 1 time annually. Choose to make your additions at the "start" rather than at the "end" of each compounding period. At this rate, your account will swell to a staggering $262,363.20 at the end of 20 years. And if you've opened this account while you're still in your 20s, you can let that $262,363.20 sit and accrue interest for an additional 20 years before you retire.

20%, however, is a remarkably high-interest rate, one that you're probably only going to find on a very risky stock market purchase. Let's look at another example that's slightly more "realistic."

Imagine that you have $1,500 to invest every 6 years, for a total of 24 years. The account that you've chosen has an interest rate of 4.3%, which is compounded quarterly. To use the compound interest calculator, begin by entering $1,500 into the principal amount, as you've just opened the account. You don't plan to invest another $1500 for another 6 years, so divide $1500/6 to determine the annual addition amount. If you do the math, you'll find that you only have to invest $250/year in order to invest $1500 into your account every 6 years.

In the compound interest calculator, enter $250 into the annual addition slot. Enter 24 under "years to grow." Enter 4.3% into the interest rate slot, and enter 4 into the slot for how many times interest is compounded annually. Choose to make additions at the "start." You'll see that, if you invest just $250 into your account over a period of 24 years, your account will swell to $14,713.13. Not a bad savings. But if you opened this account while you were still in your 20s, you now have another 20 years to let that $14,713.13 sit in your account and continue to accrue interest until you retire. To find out how much money you'll have when you're finally read to withdraw, go back to the compound interest calculator. This time, enter $14,713.13 as the principal amount. Enter "0" for the annual additions amount, as you have already invested what you wanted to invest. Leave the rest of the selected fields the same: 4.3% interest, compounded 4 times annually at the "start." Choose 20 years for the "years to grow" slot. You'll see that, if you let your savings continue to accrue interest for the next 20 years, you'll have $34,610.28 in your account when it comes time for you to retire.

While moneychimp.com's and other compound interest calculators greatly simplify the math involved in understanding how much you have to make from a potential investment, when choosing where to invest their money, many investors simply use the Rule of 72 to determine where and how to make the most money possible on their investments (Elkins, 2020).

The Rule of 72 focuses on one specific component of the compound interest formula, and that's the interest rate itself. As you may have intuited, the higher your interest rate, the faster your investment will begin to make money, while a lower interest rate will only make you money if you have a long time to let your money sit and accrue (Elkins, 2020).

The Rule of 72 is as follows: 72/interest rate=years to double. If you plug your interest rate into this formula, it will tell you how many years it will take, at your current interest rate, for the money you've invested to double. This rule stands no matter how much money you initially invest. So if you're planning to invest $10,000, the Rule of 72 will tell you how long you'll have to wait at your current interest rate to earn $20,000.

The rule is based on a 1% interest rate. So if you open an account with an APY of 1%, it will take 72 years for you to double your money. An APY of 3%, on the other hand, will only take 24 years to double, as 72/3=24. An APY of 6% will only take 12 years to double, etc. When using the Rule of 72, remember that the "interest rate" that you're entering into the formula is the amount of interest you can expect to accrue in an entire year, or 365-day period. So if your account accrues interest twice a year or quarterly at a rate of 1%, then 1% isn't necessarily the amount of interest you can expect to accrue over the course of an entire year. This is why the more frequently your account compounds interest, the more money you stand to make.

The Rule of 72 also helps to make it clear why a standard US savings account is probably not going to cut it for the average investor. The average APY of a US Savings account today is 0.09%. According to the Rule of 72, it will take 800 years for your invested money to double at that rate. You'll still be making money, but not nearly as much as you could be making if you chose to invest that money elsewhere.

Those with a great deal of money ready to invest often choose to invest in a high-yield savings account or a certificate of deposit, both of which typically offer interest rates around 2.49%, significantly higher than the average APY of a standard savings account. However, these accounts rarely prove profitable for those who don't have a large sum of money to invest initially, or who don't have the funds to make large regular investments over the course of several years.

If you invest your money in the stock market, on the other hand, whether it's through an employer-sponsored 401(k) account, a traditional Roth IRA, or an individual brokerage account, you're almost guaranteed to make much bigger returns, no matter how small your investments are. The average annualized total return over the past 90 years for S&P 500 accounts is 9.8%. And if you adjust that number for inflation, the return percentage still hovers between 7-8%. Plug 7% into the Rule of 72, and you'll see that it would take just over 10 years for your money to double (Elkins, 2020).

To go back to our previous example, let's imagine that you choose to invest your money in the stock market rather than a standard savings account. Imagine that you choose to invest in an S&P 500 account, and your average growth rate every year is 7%. Using the Rule of 72, you know that it will take a little over 10 years for your money to double at this rate. So imagine that you make an initial investment of $1,500, with the plan to invest an additional $250/year for the next 24 years. At 7% interest compounded annually, your account will grow to $23,170.81 after 24 years (Elkins, 2020).

Another interesting exercise is to plug the interest rates of your credit cards, car loans, mortgage, or student loans into the Rule of 72 to see just how much money your outstanding debt is earning your creditors. Remember that the average annual interest rate for a standard US savings account is only 0.09%. But the average annual interest rate for a credit card in the United States is 17.3%. At that rate, it will only take 4.16 years for the bank to earn back *double* what you initially charged on the card. And with a credit card or any other kind of loan, that extra money is coming out of your pocket. The reason that a low-interest rate on a loan is the same reason that a high-interest rate on an investment account is desirable - time.

Applying the Rule of 72 to future financial decisions can save you quite a bit of money, whether you're looking to take out a loan or invest your money. The Rule of 72 can help you determine what a reasonable interest rate is, and prevent you from falling prey to financial gimmicks from potential creditors or investing your money in accounts that ultimately aren't going to earn you that much money.

## Berkshire Hathaway and Compound Interest

Wall Sreet, in New York City, is home to the New York Stock Exchange (NYSE).

Weissenberger, P. (n.d.). *Greyscale photo of wall st. signage* [photograph]. Retrieved from https://unsplash.com/photos/uJhgEXPqSPk

Warren Buffett is undoubtedly one of the globe's most successful investors. In fact, a total net worth of $88.9 billion places him at the fourth-wealthiest person on the planet. While CEO of the investment bank Berkshire Hathaway, he made his investors an unprecedented 2 million percent return on their money over the course of his 52-year career. To translate that into real numbers, if you invested $10,000 into Berkshire Hathaway in 1965, your investment would now be worth $88 million (MacKay, 2020).

Undoubtedly, 1965 was a long time ago. But growing an investment by that much is almost unheard of. Warren Buffett's secret, as he himself has said many times, is playing the long-game. He never expects to make himself or his investors money overnight. He understands that, while compound interest is powerful, it's a lot more powerful over a long period of time (MacKay, 2020).

Compound interest is a "snowball" effect. The more money you have in your account, the more money you make. It's a deceptively simple idea, so simple that it's often overlooked or never considered at all by the average investor. In the words of Albert Einstein, compound interest is what makes the world go round. "He who understands it, earns it… he who doesn't… pays it."

Buffett is the star example of playing the long game because he started investing much earlier than most people. According to him, the book that changed his life was called *One Hundred Ways to Make $1,000*, a title that he found in the public library in his hometown of Omaha, Nebraska at age 7. Inspired by this book, he started his first business selling chewing gum, Coca-Cola bottles, and magazines door-to-door in his neighborhood. In middle school, he got a job working in his grandfather's grocery store. Using the money he earned at the grocery store, he bought his first stock at the tender age of 11. Specifically, he purchased three shares of Cities Service stock for himself, and three for his sister Doris Buffett. He was inspired to do so after a visit to the New York Stock Exchange with his family the year before.

In high school, he invested the money he earned delivering newspapers into a business owned by his father. He earned his spending money selling golf balls and stamps, as well as detailing cars. As a sophomore in high school, he got into business with a friend purchasing used pinball machines and then selling them to local businesses. When he graduated from Woodrow Wilson High School in Washington, D.C. in the year 1947, the tagline under his senior yearbook pictures reads "likes math; a future stockbroker."

That same year, between the stocks he had purchased when he was 11 and the money he had invested in his father's business, he had already managed to accumulate a savings of $9,800, roughly $105,000 in today's money. And because his money has been accruing interest for so long, he's managed to earn back 99% of his wealth since his 50th birthday. The interest that he's making on his investments is earning him hundreds of thousands of dollars every day, but it's because he started investing so early in his life (MacKay, 2020).

Buffett began his career as an investor in 1954, working under Benjamin Graham, the investor who invented the Mr. Market analogy for understanding stock market psychology. According to him, Graham was an extremely tough person to work for, demanding that all the company's stocks provide a wide margin of safety in addition to a high rate of annual return. Buffett's starting salary at Graham's company was $12,000 a year, about $114,000 today.

After just two years, Graham closed up his partnership, but during that time, Buffett had been investing his money. In 1956, he had accrued a personal savings of $174,000, worth about $1.64 million today. He used a portion of this money to start his own hedge-fund like investment business called Buffett Partners Ltd. He ran for Buffett Partners Ltd. for 14 years. By 1962, Buffett's partnerships were collectively worth more than $7 million, of which more than $1 million belonged to Buffett himself. Eventually, he merged Buffett Partners Ltd. with a few other partnerships to form Berkshire Hathaway, the company where he would remain CEO for the next 52 years (MacKay, 2020).

It was during his time at the head of Berkshire Hathaway that he began teaching others how to invest their money in smart and secure ways. During this time, his investments were continuing to accrue interest, making him hundreds of thousands of dollars every year. But in order to let his money continue to grow, he let his investments sit, and lived solely off of his annual salary of $50,000/year. By the year 1990, Buffett would be worth over a billion dollars. In 2008, Buffett became the richest man in the world, overtaking Bill Gates for the top spot.

While Gates managed to reclaim his crown in 2009, the power of Buffett's investments is not to be underestimated. In August 2014, a single Berkshire Hathaway share was valued at $200,000, and the price hasn't fallen far since. Over the years, he's become an incredibly popular and respected investment coach, partly because of his success, but partly because of the unique way he uses stories to illustrate abstract investment concepts (MacKay, 2020).

One such story refers to Queen Isabella's choice to fund Christopher Columbus' voyage to the New World. This kind of investment, he jokingly states, was quite risky indeed, more of a speculative venture than a sound investment. Had she chosen to deposit the $30,000 worth of today's money that she used to fund Columbus' expedition into an investment account instead, at an annual interest rate of 4%, the nation of Spain would be worth over $7 trillion from that account alone. Such is the power of compound interest (Miller, 2016).

Another historical example Buffett commonly uses is the story of King Francis, who chose to commission the painting of the Mona Lisa in 1516. In today's money, the king paid Leonardo da Vinci about $20,000 for the painting. Had he chosen to invest that money at an annual interest rate of 6%, the nation of Italy would be worth more than $1 quadrillion from that account alone. Buffett regularly used both of these examples to discourage the idea that speculative investments, including high-risk business ventures, art, and property investments, can earn investors more money than traditional stock market purchases or retirement accounts (Miller, 2016).

It's not a sexy answer to the question of earning money. Smart investing is slow work, there's no doubt about it. But the trick behind compound interest is that, while it works at a slow pace, it doesn't necessarily work at a steady one. In the beginning, your money will grow slowly, because you don't have as much principal in your account. But as the principal sum in your account grows, the more interest you make. And the more interest you make, the more interest you make on that interest. Before you know it, it's taking just a few years to double your initial investment amount, when it took you 10 or even 20 years to double it the first time (Miller, 2016).

Investing your money doesn't just help you to save - it helps you to earn. Invested money works for you while it's sitting in its account accruing interest. Think of it like an athlete training and perfecting his technique. It might take him 28 years of training to finally win a gold medal in the Olympics, but every year that he competes, he's compounding the work that he put in last year, and the year before, and the year before. His strength and skill don't increase at a steady rate. His experience increases his strength and skill exponentially every time he competes.

To look at yet another of Buffett's common financial anecdotes, let's go back to the year 1626. This is the year that the Manhattan Indigenous Nation sold their island home to a Dutch explorer named Peter Minuit for the price of $24. In 1965, the first time Buffett told this story, he estimated the land value of the island at that time to be around $12.5 billion. This, he calculated, worked out to be an annual gain of 6.12%. While this is hardly a bad interest rate, he calculates that, had what he calls the "Tribal Mutual Fund" managed to earn back 6.5% per year, their initial $24 would now be worth $42 billion. And had they managed to earn back 7%, that value makes a huge leap up to $205 billion.

This story doesn't just demonstrate the power of compound interest, but it demonstrates just how much money even a 0.4% increase in annual returns can make the investor. Half a percentage point won't matter much in the short term. But over time, it can quickly grow to be worth hundreds of thousands of dollars every year. As always, the key ingredients are time and patience. The longer you have to wait, the more money every single percentage point will make you, year after year (Miller, 2016).

# Chapter 3: Understanding the Game's Landscape

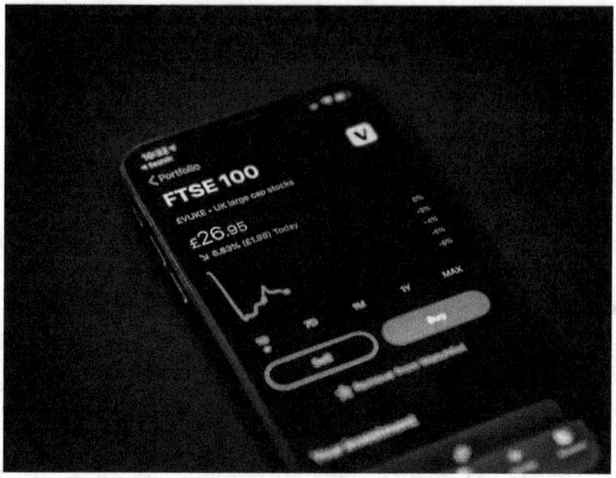


Don't move stock until you're retired, or ready to draw out on your investments.

Street, J. (n.d.). *black android smartphone on brown wooden table* [photograph]. Retrieved from https://unsplash.com/photos/VP4WmibxvcY

Before you jump into the world of the stock market, there are a few rules you'll have to learn. Too many people approach investment as a game, choosing where they place their money based on hot tips or rumors that they hear from friends or coworkers. There's a reason that people speak regularly about "playing" the stock market.

But if the stock market is a game, then it's one with clear rules and a series of strategies that have been proven to give investors an edge. Though the overall movement of the marketplace is essentially unpredictable, there is a science to understanding which kinds of investments are lower- or higher-risk. Certain patterns or trends can be followed to give you an idea of which stocks are going to be more or less profitable for the long haul. If you can learn how to "read" the stock market as it fluctuates over time, then you'll have far more success than those who just blindly invest based on rumor or advice they get from others (Edwards, 2016).

Another barrier to smart investing for many people is learning the terminology. For those just getting started, it can feel like investors are speaking an entirely different language, dropping complex words that they don't understand. But complex words don't necessarily mean complex concepts, especially when it comes to finances. This chapter will include a stock market glossary for easy reference. As you start investing your own money, any time you encounter a word you don't know, you can simply refer to the glossary for clarity. The more comfortable you are with investing and the stock market, the more comfortable you'll become using its unique language (Edwards, 2016).

If you want to play the stock market with efficiency and success, there are 8 simple rules of basic money management to follow:

1. **Borrow wisely, if at all.**

The line between "good" debt and "bad" debt is thin, but most of us don't realize that until it's too late. In an increasingly debt and credit-based economy, it's almost impossible not to borrow at some point. But the longer you can hold out, the better off you will be financially.

Debt is the opposite of investing. Any money that you gain from investments should always be weighed against the money you're losing in interest payments on your loans. At the very least, investing should be helping you to break even. But in the long-run, the less debt you have, the more money you stand to earn from the interest you accrue on your investments (Edwards, 2016).

"Good" debt are the often-necessary loans that give you access to social mobility. These are things like student and business loans, things that will ultimately put you in a better place in which to make more of your own money. Though you may have to go into debt to put yourself in a place in which to start making real money, the more financially secure you become, the better able you will be to manage and eventually pay-off your debts with your own money. The more of your debts you can manage on your own, the more money you stand to gain from smart investments (Edwards, 2016).

"Bad" debt, on the other hand, is debt that has no long-term positive impact on your financial or life situations. Credit cards firmly fall into this category, as do "payday" loans. If you don't need it, don't borrow in order to get it. You don't want all of your carefully gathered savings to go to maxed out credit cards or payments on auto loans for a car that you no longer drive. To keep things in perspective, always weigh potential debt against your current investments. If the interest you stand to pay per year on a potential loan outweighs the interest you're making per year in investment returns, then it's probably not worth it.

2. **Save from the top.**

Think of investments as a savings, not as extra money. The more money you invest, the more money you stand to make. So don't wait to invest when you have the extra money to spare. Budget regular investment payments out of your weekly or monthly paychecks. In the words of Warren Buffett, don't save what you have left after spending; spend what you have left after saving.

Of course, it's counterproductive to prioritize savings over regular bills and debt, and for many of us, there's very little left over once those two things are taken care of every month. When you don't have much money to work with, it's too easy to convince yourself that you "don't have enough" to save, or that you'll start saving when you start making more money. This mentality is incredibly financially toxic, as it prevents you from investing as early as you possibly can.

Don't think about savings in terms of dollar amounts. Instead, take a look at your monthly or weekly paycheck. Commit to investing just 1% of that check, no matter how much it is. If 1% of your check is $200, great. If 1% is just $2.00, then make that your regular investment amount. The dollar amount, as we've seen, is far less important than how long those dollars accrue interest. Beginning with 1% will get you started, and get you in the habit of regularly saving. That way, your mentality will no longer be "when I have money, I'll save" and become "when I have money, I'll save *more.*"

3. **Develop good financial habits.**

As in any other area of life, we develop certain financial behaviors that quickly turn into habits if we aren't aware of them. Financial habits are related to other areas of our lifestyle. Take a look at your bank statements monthly. Where are you spending most of your money? Is it possible to reduce that spending and save it instead? A good trick is to look back at your statements for the previous month. What was your smallest purchase that month? A cup of coffee? A book on Amazon? A meal from the fast food place down the street? Whatever it was, commit to investing the money that you would have spent, and find free or reduced-cost ways to satisfy the same lifestyle needs. If your lowest purchase was coffee, determine how many cups you purchase in a month. Once a day? Twice? Buy yourself a bag of coffee grounds from the grocery store, and make a daily investment that matches the price of your Starbucks or your Dunkin' Donuts. After a month, you'll be shocked at how much money you were losing, and how much extra money you've made on accrued interest by choosing to invest instead (Friedberg, 2020).

4. **End the paycheck-to-paycheck lifestyle.**

Unfortunately, it's all too easy to find yourself burning through one paycheck before the next one comes through. Once you've gotten yourself into this financial trap, it's extraordinarily difficult to bail yourself out. But it is possible (Friedberg, 2020).

The secret to avoiding this situation is budgeting. Make sure that the money you're spending never exceeds the money that you're earning. If that means you have to cut out or reduce a few unnecessary expenses, then so be it. You'll quickly find that driving a cheaper car or inviting your friends over for dinner rather than going out to the bar every weekend isn't as much of a sacrifice as you think, especially when you see how much more secure you are financially as a result. Even without investing the extra money, you're getting ahead simply by committing to spending less.

5. **Keep your investing simple.**

There's no need to go to an advisor or build a complex investing portfolio that spreads your money across multiple different accounts, nor is there a need to continually watch the stock market, ready to shift your money to the next "hot" stock at a moment's notice. Choose one or two low-cost S&P 500 index funds, where you can make a regular weekly or monthly contribution that's in-keeping with your budget. To open your first investment account, follow these five-steps to get yourself started without any hassle at all:

1. Research reputable investing companies, preferably ones that you're already familiar with, or which have been recommended to you by family and friends. Limit this research to a total of three hours' time. There's no need to spend days researching, as ultimately, the amount of money you make has a lot more to do with your investing habits than it does with the company where you choose to invest. As far as the stock market goes, reputations are almost always earned. If a company is reputable, it's for a good reason. And every day that you spend researching is a day you lose potential earnings from compound interest (Friedberg, 2020).

2. Create an account online with your chosen company (Friedberg, 2020).

3. Choose an index fund that invests in the top 500 companies and has low fees. These will be the most reliable places to send your money,

places that are almost guaranteed to weather the inevitable ups and downs of the marketplace. And of course, the lower the fees, the more money ends up in your pocket.

4. Transfer money into your investment account.

5. Make periodic investments, following a regular investment schedule for optimum results.

### 6. Invest for the long-haul.

Any and every time you choose to invest, commit to that company for the next 10 years. Smart investing doesn't happen overnight. If you're constantly buying and selling stocks, you'll never give your account enough time to accrue the interest that you need to really start earning a profit.

In this way, following the stock market can actually be detrimental to your investing habits. It's too easy to feel like you're losing money when the market goes down, and therefore too easy to make decisions based on fear and rumor than on established trends. The best way to invest is to choose two or three companies that you feel are reliable, and then automatically transfer your investments into that account every month. Regular investments will insulate your account against loss when the market is down, and ensure that you continue to earn a profit when the market is up.

### 7. Don't blindly follow investing advice.

Whether or not a market "tip" results in money has more to do with luck than with any kind of insight that your advisor may have had. There are people who devote their entire lives to studying the movement of the stock market, and while the insights you get from those people may be sound, the reality is that the marketplace is essentially unpredictable. If you lose money based off of a "hot" tip you got from a friend or read in a magazine, it doesn't just set you back in dollars - it sets your account back in time, as well.

The best rule of thumb before investing in new stock is to think about the long-game. Will this stock still be making you money in 10 years' time? If not, then it's not worth the investment. Whatever money you stand to make you're just as likely to lose when the marketplace inevitable changes course (Friedberg, 2020).

### 8. Save for the unexpected.

Don't make investments your only savings pool. Ideally, you'll have both an investment account *and* a standard savings account. In fact, having a standard savings account and one investment account actually stands to make you more money than two investment accounts and no standard savings (Friedberg, 2020).

The reason for this is that the marketplace isn't the only financial arena that's filled with unpredictability. Life is unpredictable, too. Emergencies happen. If you find yourself scrambling for cash every time something unexpected happens, then you'll be tempted to use credit or take out loans to cover your costs without blowing your budget. And the more debt you incur, the less money your investments are actually making you. The last thing you want is for years and years of compound interest to end up going toward credit cards and neutralizing outstanding loans.

## Stock Market Glossary of Terms

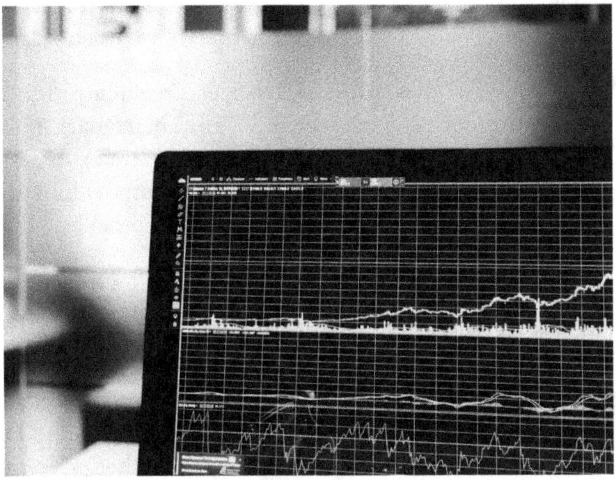

Knowing basic terms makes you an informed, smart investor.

Liverani, C. (n.d.). *turned on flat screen monitor* [photograph]. Retrieved from https://unsplash.com/photos/dBI_My696Rk

When you first start researching investing companies, you're going to encounter a lot of words that you've never seen before. Don't let this intimidate you. Stock market lingo may be confusing, but these complex-looking words rarely describe concepts that are particularly difficult to grasp. Any time you encounter a word you don't know, you can simply come back to this chapter and find it alphabetically in your personal stock market glossary of important terms.

**401k:** A retirement account set up for employees by employers, which usually allows investors to put their money to work in mutual funds or index funds. Typically, the investor gets a tax deduction at the time the account is funded, there are annual limits, employers match contributions, and there are no taxes owed until the investor begins withdrawing the money. No matter where you work or how young you are, take advantage of this benefit if your company offers it to you (Kunsman, 2020).

**403b:** A retirement account with similar rules and restrictions to a 401(k), but which is only offered for non-profit organizations (Kunsman, 2020).

**529 Plan:** A plan designed to save for future education costs. This can be set up either for K-12 tuition or for college/university costs. There are two different types of 529 plans, depending on what you're saving for (Kunsman, 2020).

**Balance Sheet:** This reports a company's assets and liabilities. It's a complete financial statement, providing a snapshot of what a company owns and what they owe, as well as the amount invested by shareholders.

**Bear Market:** A period where stock prices are falling. In this type of market, investor confidence is extremely low, and many start to sell off their stocks for fear of future losses, fueling the negative market even more. A 20% downturn or more in stock prices over a certain amount of time is the typical benchmark for a bear market. However, this kind of market can also be a great buying time, as stocks often go on sale.

**Blue Chip:** A company with a history of solid earnings, increasing dividends, and a good balance sheet.

**Bull Market:** When the market is moving in a positive direction and is expected to continue. During a bull market, optimism is high and investors tend to expect that strong results should continue, either over the next few months or even the next few years.

**Bond:** A fixed income investment in which an investor loans money typically corporate or governmental which borrows the funds for a defined period of time at a variable or fixed interest rate. There are a number of different bonds available, depending on the reason for investing.

**Book Value:** The measure of all of a company's assets, including stocks, bonds, inventory, manufacturing equipment, and real estate.

**Broker:** The entity that lets you buy and sell investments for yourself. Typically, this service incurs a fee. However, there are a growing number of discount brokers online, which often allow you to pay a flat commission per trade.

**Brokerage Account:** An account created by a licensed brokerage firm that allows an investor to add funds, after which the investor can place investment orders. The investor legally owns the assets contained in this account, but will usually have to claim any taxable income from capital gains.

**Capital Gain/Loss:** The difference between what an investor pays for an investment and the price that they sell it for. For example, purchasing a stock at $30/share and then selling it when prices have risen to $50/share would be considered a gain, while a loss would be the reverse (Kunsman, 2020).

**Commission:** A service charge assessed by a broker or investment advisor for providing investment advice or handling purchases and sales of securities for a client (Kunsman, 2020).

**Dividends:** The portion of a company's profits paid out to shareholders on a quarterly or annual basis. It's not legally mandatory for companies to pay dividends on stock, but many do to their shareholders.

**Dollar-Cost Averaging:** An investment technique of buying a certain dollar amount of a particular investment on a regular schedule, regardless of the share price. This helps to keep investments on track and is a way to minimize loss incurred by marketplace fluctuations.

**Dow Jones:** The full title is the Dow Jones Industrial Average. This number is a price-weighted average of 30 significant stocks traded on the New York Stock Exchange and NASDAQ. First invented in 1896.

**ETF:** Stands for Exchange-Traded Funds. These are like mutual funds, except that they trade throughout the day on stock exchanges as if they were individual stocks. They can hold various assets, including stocks, commodities, and/or bonds.

**Hedge Fund:** A type of investment partnership. Partners pool money from investors to engage in a wide variety of investing activities. Essentially, hedge funds are designed to manage where the money from investors ultimately goes. These can potentially be very risky for investors.

**Hidden Fees:** Many investment advisors charge fees rather than commissions. Some charge both. Often, advisors on mutual-funds will subtract payment for services directly from fund assets, which are not typically charged or advertised as "advisor fees." Though advisors are legally required to disclose fees, the fee structure can sometimes be buried in the contract or prospectus with the hope that the investor will overlook or not understand the reality of the fee costs until it's too late. These kinds of buried fee structures are often referred to as "hidden fees," and are important to watch for when opening a new investment account or seeking financial advice for a price.

**Index Fund:** A mutual fund that allows an individual to "invest" in an index, such as the S&P 500. Index funds work the same way that regular mutual funds do, but often have much lower fees. If you're looking for a stable, long-term place to invest your money, this is the place to do it (Kunsman, 2020).

**Market CAP:** A number calculated by multiplying the current price per share by the number of shares "outstanding," or those owned by investors (Kunsman, 2020).

**Market Correction:** A decline of 10% or more in the price of a security from its most recent peak.

**Market's Cyclical Movement:** The ways in which the prices of individual stocks are affected by macroeconomic or systematic changes in the overall economy.

**Money Market:** This type of investment account is an interest-bearing account that will typically pay a higher interest rate than a bank savings account would. Therefore, savings stored in this kind of account will often yield a much better monthly return than the same amount invested in a standard savings account.

**Mutual Fund:** A pooled portfolio. The fund itself holds the individual stocks or bonds, depending on where you're investing. Mutual funds are a great choice for first-time investors. However, beware of high fees. When in doubt, cross-reference the listed fees against those listed by other accounts.

**NASDAQ:** A marketplace for buying and selling securities. Thousands of stocks are listed on the NASDAQ exchange, including giant companies like Apple, Google, Microsoft, Oracle, Amazon, and Intel.

**New York Stock Exchange:** A stock exchange located in New York City that is considered the largest equities-based exchange in the world, made up of 21 rooms that are used to facilitate trading.

**P/B Ratio:** Stands for the Price-to-Book Ratio. This is a financial ratio used to compare a company's current market price to its book value.

**P/E Ratio:** Stands for the Price-Earnings Ratio. This is the ratio of a company's share price to the company's earnings per share.

**Penny Stocks:** Originally used to describe stocks that sell for less than $1/share, the term now refers to stocks that sell for less than $5/share. There are a number of risks associated with penny stocks that make many investors want to steer clear as they are extremely volatile. Though there are many success stories about investing in penny stock, there are far more stories of failure.

**Price vs. Value:** This is a comparison made between a stock's listed price and its intrinsic value. The price only tells you a company's current value, sometimes called its "market value." The intrinsic value, on the other hand, is the company's actual worth in dollars (Kunsman, 2020).

**Real Estate:** Property, such as land, houses, buildings, or garages that the owner can use or allow others to use in exchange for payment in rent. These properties are sometimes flipped for profit rather than rented out (Kunsman, 2020).

**Real Estate Crowdfunding:** A relatively new way to invest in real estate. Essentially, it gives investors the opportunity to invest in certain real estate markets that were previously off-limits, such as commercial real estate. These investments don't necessarily follow the stock market and are not as liquid, meaning you can't always get your cash back when you want to.

**REITs:** Stands for Real Estate Investment Trusts. These trusts trade as if they were stocks and have special tax treatment. There are many different types of REITs out there, depending on the kind of real estate you're looking to invest in. They often trade on major exchanges like other stocks, so they move with the market.

**Roth IRA:** An individual retirement account designed for the investor to have a place to set aside after-tax income. These kinds of accounts offer tax deductions of up to $5,500 a year for those younger than 50, and up to $6,500 for those aged 50 and older. Investors are not taxed when they begin withdrawing funds. However, there are certain limitations based on the investor's salary at the time of retirement.

**Rollover IRA:** When an employee leaves their employer, they can opt to rollover the 401(k) balance and have it deposited into a Rollover IRA, whose rules and restrictions are nearly identical to those of a Traditional IRA.

**SEP-IRA:** An IRA account that can be used by self-employed people and small business owners under certain circumstances. As with most IRAs, it comes with contribution limits, but those limits are much higher than those for a Traditional or Roth IRA.

**Simple IRA:** An IRA account for small business owners with fewer than 100 employees who want to offer some sort of retirement benefits to their employees but don't want to (or can't) deal with the rules and restrictions that come with a 401(k).

**Stocks:** Sometimes called "shares" or "equity," stocks are a type of security that signify ownership in a corporation and represent a claim on part of the corporation's assets and earnings. Most stocks are divided into two main types: common and preferred.

**Stock Broker:** An institution or individual that executes buy or sell orders on behalf of a customer, helping to settle the trades (Kunsman, 2020).

**Traditional IRA:** An individual retirement account that offers tax advantages to savers. The investor doesn't pay any taxes up front, but often will once they begin withdrawing funds. These kinds of accounts offer tax deductions of up to $5,500 a year for those younger than 50, and up to $6,500 for those aged 50 and older (Kunsman, 2020).

**Volatility:** Big swings in either direction of the stock market or individual stocks. When the stock market rises or falls more than 1% over a consistent period of time, this is typically enough to consider the market "volatile."

**Volume:** The number of shares being traded in the market during a given period of time. Every transaction that happens during trading hours contributes to the count of total volume.

**What the Timeless Investment Strategy is all About**

Vision, A. (n.d.). *shallow focus photograph of black and grey compass* [photograph]. Retrieved from https://unsplash.com/photos/uCMKx2H1Y38

The essence of the timeless investment strategy is to purchase stock in a low-cost index fund and use the dollar-cost averaging strategy to increase your earnings via compound interest for as many years as you possibly can.

At this point, it's clear that the magic of investing in the stock market is the ability to let your money sit and watch it grow. While there are a number of different ways to do this, the timeless investment strategy is nearly guaranteed to make you a significant return on your investments. The earlier you start investing, the more you stand to gain (Serwer, 2019).

This investment strategy includes the word "time" for a reason - it's not a get-rich-quick scheme. But while this investment strategy won't make you money fast, it will make you a lot *more* money if you have the patience to wait. Consider an example that Warren Buffett often gives in talks about his success as an investor. Buffett purchased his first stock at the age of 11, for a total cost of $114 that he had earned and saved shoveling snow for his neighbors. Buffet estimates that if he had invested that money into the S&P 500 in 1942, his $114 would have grown to $400,000 today. Granted, 1942 was almost 80 years ago, but it's a testament to how much money regular investments in an S&P 500 index fund can actually make you within one lifetime. This strategy is about saving money that will double and triple over time, ensuring that when you retire, your years of hard work really do pay off (Serwer, 2019).

S&P 500 index funds are the best place to put your money long-term because they're reliable. They'll weather the storm of the marketplace's continuous ups and downs. These are companies that are unlikely to go bankrupt within your lifetime, making your money as safe as you can reasonably expect it to be. And the stability relieves you of the responsibility of watching the market to determine whether or not your investment is going to be profitable. The dollar-cost averaging strategy will provide you an additional layer of protection from the market's fluctuations, and provide you with a way to make regular investments regardless of income (Serwer, 2019).

This strategy is simple enough that you shouldn't need to pay advisors or hedge funds to manage your money for you, which will save you even more money in service, management, or brokerage fees. S&P 500 companies are so stable that you can also reasonably expect to make a similar amount of return every pay period. And that return is quite high, hovering around 10% depending on the strength of the market. Imagine the compound interest that you could potentially accrue on an investment that's reliably earning 10% a year for 20 years or more.

The first component of the timeless investment strategy is choosing where you're going to invest your money. I recommend the S&P 500 because even the lowest performers in this index are among the strongest financial players in the world. Many of the companies in the index have been in business for years. Though the market has seen some huge dips and leaps in recent years, especially in response to an increasingly volatile global economy, these companies have remained relatively stable. Their prodigious resources, earnings, and assets mean that it would take a truly catastrophic disaster to bankrupt them. If that happens, then you'll probably have a lot more pressing concerns than your retirement anyway.

S&P 500 isn't the only major financial index where it's possible to open a fund. Dow Jones, NASDAQ, Global Dow, Gold, and Oil are all global index funds that are open to investor money. However, of these major indexes, S&P 500 is typically the most reliable because it's the most insulated from global economic changes. Considering how rapidly the global economy has been shifting in recent years, this kind of reliability is especially important for today's investors to consider. If you find yourself with extra money that you can stand to lose, you can try your hand at one of these other indices. But for a reliable retirement savings, I (and other investors) would recommend sticking with the S&P 500.

The second step in the timeless investment strategy is putting yourself on a regular investment schedule. I've found that people have the most success investing directly from their paychecks. If you get paid weekly, make weekly investments. If you get paid monthly, make monthly investments. This will help you to determine a regular investment amount that works for you, and reflects your current budget. Remember that you can always decrease or increase the amount you invest as you wish. The most important thing, especially in the beginning, is to get yourself comfortable making habitual investments on a regular time schedule (Serwer, 2019).

That being said, the more consistent you can be with the amount of money you make per investment, the more the dollar-cost averaging strategy will work in your favor. The strategy is meant to neutralize the effects of market fluctuation by allowing you to purchase more stock when the market is down, that you will then reap earnings and interest from when the market rises. Changing the amount that you invest, however, introduces a new variable into your investment strategy that could potentially change how much you make.

For example, if you make a smaller investment at a time when the market happens to be up, you're significantly reducing the amount of stock you're able to purchase at the time, and therefore losing potential gains in the future. If at all possible, commit to a minimum investment amount that you won't deviate from unless some kind of emergency circumstance prevents you from investing that money without compromising your financial security. Since you've opened a long-term account, it certainly won't hurt you to be able to increase your investments. But you don't want your own financial fluctuations to be compounded with the marketplace's volatility. The only weapon you have against the marketplace's unpredictability is consistency (Serwer, 2019).

The third and final component of the timeless investment strategy is time itself. The earlier you can begin investing, the more you stand to earn from compound interest over time. If you are in your early 20s, you're at the ideal age to begin investing. Using the dollar-cost averaging strategy, you can set your investment amount as low as you need to in order to get yourself started. Over the years, even the most minuscule of regular investments will grow to significant amounts.

Better still, the earlier you start saving, the earlier you can stop saving. If you open a retirement account in your early 20s, you can stop saving in your early 40s and continue to reap the interest on those savings for an additional 20-30 years before you retire. The later you start saving, the more money you potentially lose in accrued interest. Even if you continue to save right up until the moment of retirement, you'll miss out on the chance to earn years of interest on your savings.

Remember, however, that even the most frugal of savers won't earn much if they don't develop good financial habits. While you're saving up for retirement, don't rely on the money in your investment account to support you when you reach the age of 65. The less debt you have, the better. The more you can pay for with your own money, the more secure you will be. And the more rollover you have from paycheck to paycheck, the less vulnerable you will be to financial emergencies. Investments should be made with the understanding that you are not going to see that money again until you retire, which may not be for another 40+ years. Investment money is something that's ensuring a financially secure future, but that won't mean much if you don't have a financially secure present (Serwer, 2019).

The secret to financial security is a good budget. Though everyone has unique financial pressures that may stop them from having the ideal budget breakdown, the closer you can get to the recommended ratios, the better. The best way to think about your budget is not in terms of dollar amounts, but in terms of percentages (Serwer, 2019).

The ideal recommended budget breakdown is commonly referred to as the 50/30/20 budget. To make this budget, you'll first need to know the exact amount of your monthly or weekly income after taxes. Don't calculate your income based on how much you earn, calculate your income based on how much you'll take home after taxes or other automatic deductions have been accounted for.

Of the remaining amount, the 50/30/20 method dictates that roughly 50% of your regular income (weekly or monthly, depending on how you wish to divide it and/or how often you actually get paid) goes to necessities, 30% is allocated to wants, and 20% goes to savings and/or debt repayment.

To break this down even further, necessities include items like groceries, housing, utilities, transportation, minimum loan payments, child care, and/or necessary work-related expenses. In other words, these are the expenses that you (literally) can't afford to miss each month without serious negative repercussions to your personal health, safety, or security. If you are paying out-of-pocket for your own medical costs, then these should be included under necessities as well. If your calculated expenditures for these categories significantly exceeds 50% of your income, then an emergency adjustment must be made in terms of either your income amount or how much you're spending in necessities. Is there a way to reduce the cost of any of these necessities? Is there a way for you to earn more income? If necessities are taking up more than 50% of your income, then it will be nearly impossible for you to avoid living paycheck-to-paycheck, severely compromising your financial security and making it difficult for you to commit to a regular investment schedule (Serwer, 2019).

20% of your income, ideally, will go to savings and debt repayment. Remember that this is payments on loans or credit cards *above* the minimum. To make this breakdown simple, divide this portion of your income in half. Split 10% between your loan accounts, and split the other 10% between your regular savings account and your investment accounts. If you follow this budgeting method, you'll only have to spare 5% of your income to put toward your investments. But you can do so secure in the knowledge that a mere 5% of your weekly or monthly income will swell to potentially hundreds of times its size by the time you retire (Serwer, 2019).

# Chapter 4: Becoming the 10%

By keeping your cool, you can make money in the stock market.

Muza, C. (n.d.). *laptop computer on glass top table* [photograph]. Retrieved from https://unsplash.com/photos/hpjSkU2UYSU

An astonishing 90% of investors lose money on their investments. However, this is rarely due to the nature of the investment itself. Psychology, emotional stability (or lack thereof) lack of discipline, greed, and fear all play a part in whether or not an investment is successful. Though finances are based in numbers in and logic, you also have to remember that there are real, human people behind those numbers. People who are emotionally vulnerable to the natural fluctuations of the market, and who are tempted to behave in reactive, emotional ways to what they see from the market's behavior.

A true investment master doesn't let their emotions influence their decisions. But this is much easier said than done. Investment is a lifelong journey, especially those who are investing for retirement and not planning on making money overnight. Therefore, it takes a great deal of patience, discipline, and mental strength to prevent yourself from making rash, reactionary decisions based on the market, especially if you are a first-time investor.

To insulate yourself against rash, emotional decisions, you have to first try to take an objective look at your beliefs. "If I had money, it would mean…" or "People with money are…" are two thought patterns to pay close attention to. Often, our understanding of how to make money investing is based on personal stereotypes of what it means to be someone with money. Our world is one where economic disparity is not only expected, but is intentionally propagated. Certain demographics of people are expected to do well, while others are intentionally left in the dark. Certain kinds of people are taught how to manage their money, while others are intentionally left to figure it 0ut on their own. For the most part, the gap between those who have money and those who don't is intentional. Certain people in certain situations are privy to knowledge that others are purposefully excluded from (Housel, 2018).

But that is no longer the case. No matter who you are or how much money you have to invest, you have a moment now to consider why you want to invest, and what kind of person you think you will be when you withdraw that money at age 65. Question your beliefs about what it means to be a wealthy person, because if you weren't raised with money, then it's very likely that the beliefs you carry are based more on stereotypes than they are on reality (Housel, 2018).

In many ways, there is an all-to-real gap between rich and poor. But in other ways, this gap is psychologically manufactured. The cycle of poverty is partly historically based, and partly psychologically based (Housel, 2018). To illustrate the point, let's take a look at an example.

Meet Grace Groner. She was orphaned at age 12. She never married, had children, or owned a car. She lived most of her life in a one-bedroom home, working her entire career as a secretary. Would you like to guess how much she was worth when she died? Would you be surprised to know that she was a millionaire who left all $7 million to charity after she died in 2010 at the ripe old age of 100? If you're like most people, it would surprise you. How, you might ask, did she manage to earn all of that money? The answer? The stock market.

While she saved her money, spent frugally, and invested wisely in the stock market, her net worth continued to grow over time. When she retired, she was financially secure enough to have an excess amount of $7 million dollars to donate to the causes she believed in when she died. There was no inheritance. No mystery relative swooping in to donate thousands to her account. She just invested. Smartly. And that's what made her millions (Housel, 2018).

By contrast, let's look at Richard Fuscone. Once upon a time, he was vice chairman of Merrill Lynch's Latin America division. He was educated at both Harvard University and the University of Chicago. In his 40s, he was such a successful investor that he retired in order to pursue both "personal and charitable interests." But high debts and unwise investments forced him to ultimately declare bankruptcy, fighting off foreclosure on two homes, one of which had a $66,000 a month mortgage payment (Housel, 2018).

This is hardly a morality tale, telling you to be more like Grace and less like Richard. Instead, it's a reality check. Only in the world of finances can the story of Grace and Richard exist in the same industry. You will never hear a tale of the self-taught Grace Groner performing brain surgery better than the Harvard-educated Richard. How well you do financially has nothing to do with how smart you are, and everything to do with how *disciplined* you are. It has a lot more to do with why you're saving your money, and a lot less to do with how much money you're saving.

Here's something to consider as a first time investor: **the earned success and deserved failure fallacy.** Too many people ignore the very real role that luck and risk have to play in any financial decision. Luck and risk are essentially two sides of the same coin. If you succeed at a risky venture, that has a lot more to do with luck than it does with your intelligence or financial wherewithal when it comes to investing in that particular company. And the opposite is also true. Extremely intelligent people make very bad investments all the time. It has nothing to do with their intelligence, and everything to do with the unpredictability of the market.

It's almost taboo to talk about luck in financial contexts. Anyone who wishes to remind the average investor that they have just as much to gain from luck as they do from intelligent investing is considered a pessimist at best, and a cynic or a troublemaker at worst. But if you believe that luck has a great deal to do with the success of your investment, then you're actually being more realistic than a number of investors putting thousands of dollars into companies that they've been "tipped off" will make them a profit. The market is essentially unpredictable. You can't accept that and deny the power of luck in any profit that you subsequently make (Housel, 2018).

The opposite is also true. When investors lose money, they look for someone to blame. Did the companies they invested in not try hard enough? Did they not think their investments through enough? Perhaps they were just too lazy to do the appropriate amount of research? But the reality is that the market is… you guessed it, unpredictable. Sometimes the investment that made the most "sense" at the time turns out to be a very bad choice indeed. No one can know for certain, because no one can predict the future. We can make reasonable assumptions based on past data. This is the reason that the timeless investment strategy suggests you invest in S&P 500 companies rather than in other index funds. However, investing in an S&P 500 company is no guarantee of wild success. The smart investor understands that an investment includes risk. Always. Even smart investments come with some possibility of loss (Housel, 2018).

Just as much of the market's fluctuations are driven by luck, chance, and accident as they are by predictable trends or the behavior of the businesses participating in the market. The economy is connected to human lives, which means that it's connected to human behavior. And human behavior, to put it bluntly, doesn't always make sense. It certainly doesn't always follow predictable or reliable patterns. The line between bold and reckless is much thinner than most people think, as is the line between crazy and brilliant. This is how speculators continue to make money. If they're lucky, they make a fortune. And if they're unlucky, they're bankrupt.

The timeless investment strategy, for the most part, will help you to find a middle ground between these two extremes. For the most part, regularly investing the same amount of money in a low-cost, S&P 500 index fund for 40 years will result in earnings at least triple the amount of the initial investment. But it's not a guarantee. There is no guarantee when it comes to playing the stock market. Anyone who tells you otherwise is not telling you the full truth.

Yet another psychological shortcoming to be aware of is the **cost avoidance syndrome.** This is what happens when someone fails to acknowledge the full costs of a certain investment, placing too much emphasis on emotional rewards and not considering the very real impact of emotional cost when it comes to making a profitable investment.

To fully understand this syndrome, let's look at an example. Imagine that you want a new car. The car you want costs $30,000. There are three courses of action that you can take in order to obtain this car: 1) Pay the full $30,000, 2) Buy a used one for less than $30,000, or 3) Steal it (Housel, 2018).

If you are like 99% of people, you'll automatically discount the third option. The social, emotional, and psychological costs of stealing a car far outweigh the financial rewards of not having to pay for one. This is obvious. Take this mindset into your investments. Don't expect that you're going to get future rewards back for nothing. Everything costs something. As a smart investor, what you're looking for is how to get back the most money for the lowest investment cost (Housel, 2018).

So if you want to earn high returns on your investment, you should expect that those returns aren't going to come for free. You're going to have to give something in order to get back the money that you want. *All* investment strategies require some kind of sacrifice. In the case of the timeless investment strategy, the "sacrifice" that you're giving up is time. The earlier you start investing, the less painful this sacrifice is. But it is important to get out of the mindset that money earned on the stock market is "free" money.

## The Language of Successful Investors

Different indices have different trajectories. Invest regularly, no matter what.

Spiske, M. (n.d.-a). *new york times newspaper* [photograph]. Retrieved from https://unsplash.com/photos/3Tf1J8q9bBA

The first step in changing your beliefs about wealth is changing how you talk and write about wealth. Language defines how we think, just as much as how we think defines how we speak. If you say something often enough, you will eventually believe it. So even before you start to *think* like a successful investor, it's important to start speaking and writing like one.

The first rule of successful business speak is to use **conversational language.** There's no harm in expanding your vocabulary or regularly using financially charged words. But many investors can see through "corporate speak" because investing is one of the few industries where education doesn't really matter. You can write beautifully crafted letters like Warren Buffett or be barely literate. If you have good financial sense and understand that no investment is guaranteed to make money, then you're going to make a great deal playing the stock market (Lessons from Warren Buffett's Gift for Language and Storytelling, 2018).

So when you're talking to others, don't allow yourself to be intimidated by corporate- speak. Remain secure in the knowledge that regular, human, conversational language is the way that wealthy respected investors speak too. People as wealthy as Bill Gates, Warren Buffett, and Jeff Bezos have been both praised and criticized for their regular use of everyday language when they communicate about finances. Don't feel any pressure to artificially elevate your language in order to make a point, and certainly don't feel like the fact that someone is using elevated language means that they know what they're talking about when it comes to investing (Lessons from Warren Buffett's Gift for Language and Storytelling, 2018).

The point of mastering industry jargon isn't to lord it over the heads of others - it's to ensure that you don't get left out of any financial discussions. Often, the words we use when writing are very different from the words we use when speaking. The language of a Forbes article, for example, is going to be very different from the language used by real investors at a convention. The written word is inevitably more formal. Financial columns and articles are written with an elevated and academic tone with the goal of being as specific and clear as possible. But if you sound like a Forbes article when you're trying to have a casual conversation with a friend or fellow investor, the other person is probably not going to appreciate your usage of industry jargon (Lessons from Warren Buffett's Gift for Language and Storytelling, 2018).

Another rule of communication to remember is **accountability**. If you've made a mistake, or if your investment didn't go the way that you planned, own up to it. The world's top investors don't blame others for their mistakes, and neither should you. If something doesn't work out the way that you expected, learn from your mistake. When following the timeless investment strategy, you may also want to wait and see if things are really as bad as you believe. In the world of (stable) investing, what looks like a mistake can quickly turn into a success with patience and commitment.

The third rule of successful investing language is **master the anecdote.** An anecdote, simply put, is an interesting story about a real person. This story is often told with the intention of conveying some kind of message or illustrating a certain point. Warren Buffett's "Letters to Shareholders" is a prime example of this communication style when it comes to finances. When you experience something meaningful, or something that you think others could benefit from, share it. The world of finance is not one that rewards hoarders or secret keepers. The more insight you have to offer others, the more widely respected you will be.

The fourth rule of investing language is learning to master **levity**. In other words, learning to master humor. Taking your investments too seriously won't impress anyone, nor will it foster the right attitude within yourself. All of us encounter strange and unexpected situations throughout the course of our chosen investment history. The more you can learn to embrace and share these situations with humor, the better you will feel about your investment history, and the more respect your listeners will have for you (Lessons from Warren Buffett's Gift for Language and Storytelling, 2018).

**Metaphors and analogies** are examples of metaphoric language that are important for any potential investor to master. First of all, experienced investors often speak in metaphor. Let's look at a few examples from Warren Buffett, one of the world's most successful investors (Lessons from Warren Buffet's Gift for Language and Storytelling, 2018): "Every decade or so, dark clouds will fill the economic skies, and they will briefly rain gold. When downpours of that sort occur, it's imperative that we rush outdoors carrying washtubs, not teaspoons." "It's the growth of the Berkshire forest that counts. It would be foolish to focus over-intently on any single tree."

In both of these examples, Buffett is not literally talking about washtubs and trees. He's speaking about the stock market, but in metaphoric language. The more comfortable you can become using symbol and analogy to talk about finances, the better able you will be able to both communicate with masters in your field, as well as communicate to other people what your own investment goals and philosophies are.

**Word choice** is another important thing to consider when reading or communicating about one's investments. Sometimes it's important to use and understand corporate- speak. Other times, you'll want to be well-versed in the language of the stock market. And still other times… you'll want to communicate like a regular human being. The secure and successful investor will understand which circumstances warrant the use of which kind of language. Using corporate-speak to impress your family or your girlfriend probably won't. But using regular language in a board meeting may not win you any points either. The language of the successful investor changes depending on the social context. Not only is that perfectly fine, it's actually recommended if you want to start speaking like a successful investor. While it's tempting to show off the fancy new words you've learned, it's not always appropriate. Learn when and how to use industry lexicon without sounding like you're trying to impress the people you're speaking with. The more casual you sound, paradoxically, the more you'll sound like you know what you're talking about.

The bottom line is that, no matter who you're talking to or how much money your investments are worth, trying to sound like the smartest person in the room will always make it sound like you're…trying to sound like the smartest person in the room. People are rarely fooled or impressed by overly flowery language. While it's important for you to know some of the industry lingo before you start investing, it's not really that important for you to use that lingo in everyday conversation. You want to know what certain words mean when you read or hear them. But as much as possible, try to continue to communicate in a way that's humble and every day.

Unlike other industries, being the most educated person doesn't necessarily mean that you're the most respected, or even the most successful. Finance is a world of numbers and facts, and that means that, if you're going to lord yourself over others, you'd better have some real cash to back up your fancy attitude if you want people to respect you (Lessons from Warren Buffett's Gift for Language and Storytelling, 2018).

At the end of the day, it comes back to beliefs. Our language and our perceptions about what it means to be a financially secure person are tied together. If you're interested in investing because you want to be somehow better or smarter than other people, those intentions will eventually shine through. Similarly, if you want to invest in the stock market because you want to create a stable financial future for yourself, then those intentions will also be clear to others. Never forget who you are or where you come from.

Whenever you're communicating with others, remember that your net worth doesn't have any kind of bearing on what kind of person you are. There are plenty of intelligent, kind, and remarkable people who never invested a cent of their money. And the stock market is flooded with intelligent, kind, and remarkable people who simply didn't hit the lucky break they needed to save any kind of real money, or who followed financial schemes that were more risky than the one I'm presenting here in this book. Long story short, being a successful investor has nothing to do with your character. Any kind of person can be financially secure, just as any kind of person can be financially insecure. When communicating with others, don't try to impress others with your newfound wealth. Humility goes a long way. The less you try to lord your savings and security over others, the more respect others will have for your financial wherewithal (Lessons from Warren Buffett's Gift for Language and Storytelling, 2018).

Don't take what I'm saying for granted. As you watch your investment accounts start to increase in value, listen to interviews with the top five wealthiest people in the world. As of 2020, those people are Jeff Bezos, Bill Gates, Bernard Arnault, Warren Buffett, and Larry Ellison. Listening to these five individuals speak will not only give you a better idea of how the wealthy communicate, but it will also give you some great insights into how the wealthy think.

Because there's no doubt about it - language and thought are interrelated. We think the way that we speak, and we speak the way that we think. Intentionally forcing yourself to communicate in a humble, natural way will force your brain to maintain a humble, natural view of yourself, whether your network is -$10,000 or over $20,000,000. The way that you communicate defines you who are, not just from a social perspective, but from a psychological perspective. Pay attention to how you speak, and notice how your speech patterns start to change as you start to earn more money. If you notice that you're beginning to speak in jargon-rich or pretentious ways, make an effort to employ some of the humbling strategies outlined in this chapter.

The last result that you want from your newfound financial security is to alienate all of your friends and family! Keep perspective.

Remember that successful investments are just as much about luck as they are about intelligence. Give others advice when they ask for it, and allow people to make their own financial choices when they aren't offering you advice. It's ok to nod and smile when someone is trying to give you financial advice that you know isn't worth following. At the end of the day, it's up to them to make their own smart choices with their money, just as it's up to you to make your own smart choices with yours (Lessons From Warren Buffett's Gift for Language and Storytelling, 2018).

## The Habits of Successful Investors

Develop strong investing habits.

Spiske, M. (n.d.-b). *white paper with print* [photograph]. Retrieved from https://unsplash.com/photos/2VMcpbUR6w8

Finding yourself among the ranks of the top 10% of investors isn't just about beliefs and language. Successful investors have, nine times out of ten, developed certain habits that contribute to their likelihood of success in the stock market and in the world of finances in general. Excellence, more often than not, is not what we do in one important moment. Rather, excellence is a habit, something that we cultivate over time through small but significant behavior patterns.

As you now know, lifestyle habits and financial habits are often linked. After all, money is typically the way that we fuel certain lifestyle choices. Where we choose to spend (or not spend) our money often says a great deal about who we are as people. As such, it probably won't surprise you to learn that almost all successful investors have a certain cluster of traits in common. If you can master these traits in your own life, then you, too, will significantly increase your chances of becoming a successful investor (Fidelity Viewpoints, 2020a).

### Start with a Plan

Creating a financial plan is the bedrock on which success is built. Financial planning in all areas of your life will help you to understand your current situation, define your financial goals, and take the necessary steps to achieve those goals (Fidelity Viewpoints, 2020).

Financial planning is often advertised as a service, but in reality, it's a habit. You can choose to do it with the help of a professional, but planning is actually a foundational part of budgeting, and something that every human should do, regardless of what their finances look like or what their ultimate goals are. Successful investors rarely become wealthy by accident. This is why financial planning is a basic service offered by most finance professionals, but it's also something that you can easily do for yourself (Fidelity Viewpoints, 2020).

People with financial plans are significantly better able to meet long-term financial goals than those without them. Many people dream of what they want their finances to look like when they retire, but too few turn those dreams into sound plans. There is no retirement goal that is unachievable, but the longer you wait to plan and save, the more unrealistic those goals become (Fidelity Viewpoints, 2020a).

This is why good investment habits are tied to good financial habits. The way that you budget, spend, and save your earned money has a direct effect on how much and how regularly you'll be able to invest. Saving early and often is the best investment strategy, but this will be difficult for you to do if you're losing a significant portion of your income to unnecessary debts and expenses.

### Be a Super Saver

Rather than focusing on how much you're making on the market, trust in the power of compound interest to make you a significant amount of money, and focus instead on how much of your income you're currently putting away for the future. Saving early and saving often is critical to investment success.

Most advisors recommend putting between 10-15% of your income into an investment account. If you have the discipline to save more, that's great, but don't compromise your current financial security for the sake of saving for the future. If you're starting your retirement plan early, then you don't have to worry about putting away huge sums of money, as long as you get yourself on a regular investment schedule. Many financial studies suggest that 15% is the ideal number to invest for retirement, but again, if sticking to this number is going to prevent you from putting money into your emergency savings every month, then don't be afraid to invest less.

A Fidelity survey of three generations looked at the retirement investment habits of people across three different age groups. In general, the survey found that those investing more than 10% of their monthly income were able to meet their retirement goals. However, those who invested less than 10% were still able to reach as much as 80% of their retirement goals. The same study also found that baby boomers, or the generation born between 1944-1964, were only able to reach 95% of their retirement goals, even when investing more than 10% of their monthly income. Only those who had started investing before the age of 35 were able to reach more than 80%, regardless of how much of their income they invested once they started saving. Time is money in the world of investing. Starting to invest early can be just as powerful as investing large sums of money later (Fidelity Viewpoints, 2020).

At the end of the day, there is no "ideal" amount of money to invest. Trying to stretch your budget to accommodate a certain average or ratio can end up doing more harm than good. The more you can invest the better; but not if making a steep investment commitment is going to prevent you from saving for emergencies or paying back your debts. If anything, paying off your debts and investing less than 10% of your income would be the most sensible financial plan. It won't matter how much you've managed to save if those savings go straight to paying off the interest on outstanding loans (Fidelity Viewpoints, 2020).

### Diversify

"Diversification" is the practice of investing in a variety of stocks, bonds, and other assets. Having a mix of different kinds of investments can help you to control risk, especially in a market that's increasingly volatile. Diversification won't protect you from risk entirely, but is definitely a strategy to consider if you want to invest in indices beyond the S&P 500. And you don't have to just diversity between stocks, bonds, and cash - you can also diversify within those categories. For example, if you want to stick with stocks, consider investments across a variety of regions, sectors, investment styles (value, blend, or growth), and size (large, mid, and small-cap stocks). If you want to stick with bonds, you can try investing across a variety of credit qualities, maturities, and issuers.

If you choose to begin with an S&P 500 index fund, you can be relatively sure that your investment will slowly and steadily grow, regardless of the market's fluctuations. But if you want to invest in indices or other assets that are less secure, then diversification is an alternative strategy to ensure that your overall earnings are high, even in the face of unexpected marketplace highs and lows.

The smartest way to invest is to start out with an account that's relatively safe and secure. If you can, try to attach your main retirement account to a secure S&P 500 or other kind of index fund. Then, as you become more comfortable with investing and as you find yourself with more money to invest, you can start to comfortably branch out and diversify your portfolio in a natural way. Diversification is yet another strategy that is more effective with time. Trying to establish a diverse portfolio all at once can be stressful, and will almost inevitably result in a few bad investments. Diversification over time, on the other hand, means that you can make thoughtful choices. Diversifying your portfolio one account or asset at a time increases the likelihood that you'll choose to put your money in secure places, and also increases the likelihood that you'll actually stick to your investment schedule (Fidelity Viewpoints, 2020).

### Stick with your Plan

The number one way that investors lose money is bailing on their chosen assets the first time the marketplace falls. The best investors are emotionally impervious to marketplace fluctuations. Instead, they choose stocks that they can comfortably commit to for the long haul (Fidelity Viewpoints, 2020).

During the financial crisis of 2008 and 2009, the stock market dropped by nearly 50%, a tremendous dive. However, marketplace studies after the crash have unanimously proven that those who chose to stick with their investments are now much more financially well-off than those who chose to withdraw their money or move their investments elsewhere.

Specifically, from June 2008 to 2017, those who stuck to their investments saw an average growth rate of 147%. Those who chose to withdraw in 2008, on the other hand, only saw an average growth rate of 74%, even if they chose to reinvest in stocks that were more stable or more valuable. Those who made no changes to their investments in response to the marketplace's drop made double those who tried to change their strategy in the face of the downturn. More than 25% of investors who pulled out of the stock market during the crisis never reinvested at all!

Remember that anxiety is a normal and natural response to marketplace drops. However, don't let that anxiety stop you from making your regularly scheduled investments. If you continue to invest in both good times and bad, then through dollar-cost averaging, you'll end up making significantly more money when the market swings back up again.

### Consider Low-Fee Investment Products

You can't control the market, but you can absolutely control the costs you incur while setting up your investment accounts and choosing your assets. Don't be fooled by advertisements or articles that insist high-fee funds are worth the cost - they aren't. A number of studies have proven over and over again that high fees eat significantly into potential returns, even if those high fees result in high profits. There are so many low-cost funds out there, there's no reason to give up your long-earned returns to costs and fees. Investing should never be expensive (Fidelity Viewpoints, 2020).

### Focus on After-Tax Returns

While you're watching your investments grow over time, it's very easy to forget one very important aspect of investing, and that's taxes. Accounts that offer tax benefits, including 401(k)s, IRAs, and annuities will almost always result in higher returns for the investor than those that don't. While accounts without tax benefits can often yield higher profits, the investor stands to potentially lose a significant amount of those profits to taxes. Many investors practice something called "account location," which essentially means adjusting the amount of money they invest based on the tax benefits of the respective accounts (Fidelity Viewpoints, 2020).

Don't let taxes alone influence your investment decisions, but you should consider making your retirement account something tax-deferrable like a 401(k) or an IRA to ensure that you are able to keep as much of your returns as possible when it's time to withdraw. On the other hand, index funds are often a great choice for taxable accounts because they are nearly guaranteed to make the investor a profit, even after taxes have been taken out.

# Chapter 5: Truths, Philosophies, and Facts

The NYSE is one of the world's largest stock exchanges.

Vyas, A. (n.d.). *man's eye view of mansion* [photograph]. Retrieved from https://unsplash.com/photos/6Ih4UoqzaAs

It's no accident that successful investors like Warren Buffet and Ray Dalio inevitably end up with a celebrity-like following. Investing itself requires a certain mindset, one that inevitably starts to color other areas of life, even outside of finances. Investing is a kind of philosophy or personal code, something that has more to do with lifestyle choices than it does with intelligence or study. Everyone is "smart" enough to invest. There are countless stories of people who are both extremely intelligent and highly educated losing millions in bad investments.

Knowledge of the market is only one piece of the puzzle. Nine times out of ten, investors lose money because of a failing of character. Somewhere along the way, their fear or lack of discipline caused them to make a bad decision. Successful investors follow certain philosophies and make certain lifestyle adjustments because they understand that success is the result of habits and mindset, not the results of intelligence or education.

In such a nebulous field, it's difficult to differentiate "truths" from falsehoods. Often, investment truths are more abstract than those who are new to investing expect. These truths come in the form of tips from those at the top. When asked for insights into how they made the money that they did, the answers that most investors give is rarely about hard finances and almost always about what they were thinking and feeling (Whitt, 2019).

Warren Buffett is often held up as the investment ideal, and that's not only because of the amount of money he's made. His philosophical principles on how to cultivate a success mindset have been used by people in multiple industries, not just in the world of investing. As you embark on your investment journey, here are five pieces of investment wisdom that come from the master himself (Whitt, 2019).

### Invest in What You Know

Before you purchase stock in a company, take a moment to do a little research. Don't blindly invest in companies because of the price of their stock or their current popularity. Understand what your company does and how it makes its money. Become familiar with their products and services. Know who the CEO is, and what their business philosophies are. Buffett is noted for his repeated refusal to invest in tech stocks. While many people interpret this as a sign that tech is an unreliable place to make money, the truth of the matter is much more simple. Buffett never invests in tech because he doesn't understand it. He sticks to what he knows, a mindset that enables him to stick to his investment schedules and invest year after year with confidence in his chosen stocks (Whitt, 2019).

Following this logic, it makes sense that Buffett prefers to invest in Berkshire stock. Of course, Berkshire Hathaway is a company with which he is intimately familiar. Though its stocks cover a diverse range, from utilities to banking to insurance and consumer products, these are all areas and industries that Buffett himself is familiar with. He understands how these industries work, what Berkshire's role is in these industries, and what kinds of products and services they are offering in various sectors. This enables him to invest with confidence over the course of years (Whitt, 2019).

### Before Buying a Stock, List Your Criteria

In some ways, buying stocks on the basis of criteria is logical. This is the best way to ensure that you don't end up investing in something unfavorable. Looking at the stock's criteria essentially means looking for stock in a certain industry with a set price-to-earnings ratio in mind. This kind of mindset will help you to invest with intention, and not get swayed by the trends that are popular at the time that you're looking to invest.

Unfortunately, too many people use the price of the stock as the thing on which they base their ultimate decision. But price of stock is actually the least important indicator of a company's future success. Even the best companies take price dips from time to time because of the overall market situation. Holding on to these stocks can still earn you a profit when the market eventually starts to climb again. Stocks that are cheap now may be worth a great deal in a few months, or even a few years. Conversely, stocks that are placed at a high-value now may not hold on to that value in the long-run. Don't invest in the stock; invest in the company.

### Be Aggressive During Hard Times

"Timing" the market is popular investment advice, but as with most popular bits of wisdom, it's rarely good advice. If you're investing for the long-term, you'll be fine no matter when you choose to buy. Being defensive during hard times and aggressive during good times won't help you accrue higher savings in the long run. Keep looking for opportunities, in both good times and bad. Stick to your investment schedule, no matter what's going on in the greater economy. The best investors understand that the market is always changing. Good times don't last forever, and neither do dips nor recessions.

In fact, an excellent example, again, of how remaining steady is the best way to invest is the economic recession in 2008. As mentioned, the people who made it out of the recession without losing money were almost all people who made no changes to their investment plan. Those who carried on as usual, without allowing the grim market predictions to affect their investment choices, not only made it through the recession without incurring any serious losses, but have ultimately made huge profits on the stocks that they were able to buy in bulk while the market was down (Whitt, 2019).

### Don't Worry About the Day to Day Market Movements

Only buy a stock if you are comfortable holding on to it. Before you invest, imagine what the stock is going to be worth 10 years from now. Imagine that the stock market is going to be down for the next decade. Are you ready to commit to consistently buying up that low stock, patient in the knowledge that your earnings will double and triple when the market eventually turns around? If you don't have this kind of faith in the stock you're considering, don't invest. And if you do have this kind of faith in your investments, then you can rest easy at night, regardless of the day-to-day dips and jumps in the marketplace. Daily swings don't matter in the long-haul. You have time on your side, and if you've invested in a low-cost index fund, the overall trend of earnings is almost guaranteed to be going up (Whitt, 2019).

Avoid obsessively following the market, but also avoid obsessively following economy-related news. Trade wars, government shutdowns, and global economic downturns can make even the most disciplined investor feel anxious about their investments. Don't give this kind of news any credence. Time is on your side. S&P 500 companies are an almost ironclad investment. They aren't going to disappear any time soon, and have the financial stability to weather even the most severe of economic storms. Again, remember that you're investing in the company, not the stock. If the company you've invested in has a bright future, then temporary dips in market value won't affect your earnings - even if those dips seem catastrophically low.

### Buy Buffett's Stocks

If Warren Buffett isn't your favorite investor, you can follow this logic with someone else. But if you're really unsure where to invest, a great strategy is to invest in the same places that other successful investors are putting their money. The most successful people tend to keep things simple. You may be surprised to learn where the investment giants like Warren Buffett or Ray Dalio are actually making their money. And most of them publicly disclose their earnings annually, so the information is relatively easy to find. Don't invest blindly - make sure you're familiar with the company before you choose to buy stock yourself. But following this strategy can narrow down the endless possibilities available in the current market to a few companies that you know have been successfully making money for other people (Whitt, 2019).

Buffett, for example, puts almost all of his investments into big corporations that have a solid business future, including Apple, Wells Fargo, and Bank of America. You can also choose to invest in Berkshire Hathaway, or in any companies managed by CEOs that you particularly like. This method gives you the bonus of investing in both a company and a business philosophy that appeals to you (Whitt, 2019).

These five investment "rules" aren't hard and fast. You can choose to follow them, or you can choose to find your own way. All of these rules are proposed and followed by Warren Buffett, but if you wish, you can do research on the personal rules that other successful investors follow. Find someone whose truths resonate with you, and apply to your own investment strategy.

Always remember that there is no investor that got successful all by themselves. Most top investors are part of advisory networks, so that they can continue to learn and communicate with other successful people. No matter how much money you make, a successful investor understands that there's always something they can learn from others, whether it's a bit of personal wisdom, a financial management trick, or a new perspective on the market.

Like most successful investors, Warren Buffett has published a number of books and articles detailing his personal and business philosophies, most of which are widely available for purchase online or in bookstores. He has also appeared in a number of interviews with major news networks and business magazines, most of which you can watch for free on YouTube. And if Buffett himself doesn't appeal to you, there are a number of other investors who have been just as successful and just as public about sharing their investment wisdom.

If you're looking for an investing role model, check out such giants as Ray Dalio, Carl Icahn, Jack Bogle, and John Templeton. And the stock market is no longer the men's playground that it once was. If you're looking for some female role models, check out such successful investors as Suze Orman, Barbara Corcoran, Esther Dyson, J. Kelly Hoey, and Tina Sharkey.

## Ray Dalio's 3-Step Formula

Learn from other successful investors, and follow their strategy.

Nowakowski, A. (n.d.-b). *man sitting in front of the MacBook pro* [photograph]. Retrieved from https://unsplash.com/photos/D4LDw5eXhgg

One of today's investing giants and mentors is Ray Dalio, founder of Bridgewater Associates, the world's largest hedge fund. Forbes estimates that

Dalio's net worth is about $18 billion, but when he founded Bridgewater Associates in 1975, he was living in a two-bedroom apartment in New York City. Bridgewater has since returned the biggest cumulative net profit for a hedge fund *ever*, making it the largest in the world (Montag, 2019).

While Buffett offers five key strategies to the successful investor, Dalio's method is a little more simple. He boils down his investment philosophies into three simple steps, something that he calls the 3-Step Formula. Dalio swears by this method, and has mentioned it in several interviews with major news networks and business magazines. This is the way that he makes his money, the philosophy that he lives by when managing his money on the market (Montag, 2019).

### 1. Decide how Much You can Sock Away

In Dalio's mind, savings equal both freedom and security. So when determining how much you can afford to save, determine how much freedom and security you're willing to sacrifice for.

Dalio recommends asking yourself two simple questions when investing for retirement: How long can I get by on my savings without having any income? And how many months of freedom and safety do I need? The answers to these questions will help you to determine how much you want to save, what your retirement goals actually are, and what adjustments you'll have to make to your budget in order to meet those goals.

If you don't feel like you're in the financial position to reach those goals, don't be afraid to go in small steps. Remember, time is on your side. When you first start investing, calculate how much money you will need to have saved in order to have complete financial freedom and security for a full six months after you retire, living entirely off of your savings. Once you've hit that target, calculate how much you'll need to have saved for three or four years. Once you've hit that target, start thinking about the other people in your family. Do you have a partner? Children? Will they be dependent on your money? Which of their needs would you like to finance, if any? Breaking your retirement goals into these smaller, more manageable targets will help you to set goals that seem both realistic and attainable. And if you stick to your investment schedule, you'll probably find that you hit your initial six-month target much faster than you believed possible.

## 2. Create a Diversified Portfolio

Dalio actively discourages using a standard savings account to save. His reason for this is essentially twofold. First, savings accounts simply don't have high enough interest rates to make you any money. The average interest rate on a US bank account today is a pitiful 0.10%, meaning that for every dollar you save, you're only earning back 10 cents in interest. Dalio encourages investors to refer to the current consumer price index when trying to determine a reasonable interest rate for their invested funds. The consumer price index is a formula that measures the overall costs of goods and services. This index rose by 2.7% in the past year, meaning that any interest rate lower than 2.7% is actually costing you money. Whatever money you make in interest will be depleted simply by helping you survive. It's like an additional tax on your returns, something that's going to come out of your money whether you like it or not. You don't want to just survive off of your investments - you want to thrive (Montag, 2019).

Dalio recommends stocks, bonds, and real estate as the most secure assets in which to make investments for the long-term. These assets almost guarantee that you will turn a profit, one that keeps you well ahead of the inflation curve. In this way, Dalio's strategy compliments the timeless investment strategy easily. A low-cost index fund fits into his assertion that stocks are a profitable place in which to invest your money, one that will make you enough money in returns to reach your financial goals and keep as much of your money as possible when it comes time for you to start withdrawing (Montag, 2019).

However, Dalio is a big advocate for diversified portfolios, something that is definitely possible if you start investing early. Many people choose to split their investments evenly between stocks and bonds, but Dalio argues against this strategy. He feels that this kind of diversification doesn't offer enough protection against the market's natural fluctuation. His ideal portfolio would be 30% stocks, 40% long-term US bonds, 15% intermediate US bonds, 7.5% gold, and 7.5% other commodities, including real estate. He argues that this mix ensures that, no matter what's happening in the market, one of your investments is always doing well. Even if the market shrinks in one area, it's likely to be growing or remain stable in other areas, keeping your profits at an even rate of growth.

If this kind of strategy appeals to you in the long-term, then there's certainly no harm in trying this method of diversification for yourself. However, for the purposes of the timeless investment strategy, I would recommend starting simple. Choose one or two companies from a low-cost index fund, preferably the S&P 500. Get yourself on a regular investment schedule of purchasing stocks at regular intervals. For the first few years of your investing life, this will mean that 100% of your assets are in stocks. After you've gotten more comfortable as an investor and have successfully built an investment routine into your financial habits, then you can begin to branch out. I've found that diversification works best with increases in income.

If you find yourself starting to make more money, you can choose to simply increase the size of your investment payments, or you can choose to make smaller payments in another area, naturally diversifying your portfolio over time. In this way, you have one stable investment account that you can guarantee will turn you a profit over the course of the years. And along the way, each new investment account that you open is just more potential earnings on top of your stable savings core (Montag, 2019).

### 3. Learn the Market's Long-Term Cycles

While Buffett regularly advocates simply ignoring the market's fluctuations, Dalio has a slightly different approach. He argues that a good investor should understand the historic movements of the market in relation to the economy. If you understand the patterns that the market has followed in the past, then you'll be better able to make a smart decision in terms of where to put your money securely for the long-term. If you wish to diversify your portfolio over time, then this awareness of market cycles can be particularly beneficial. While your low-cost index fund is nearly guaranteed to remain stable despite the market's natural movements, this isn't necessarily the case for other kinds of investments. Understanding the market's historical responses to certain economic pressures can help you to choose companies and assets that will be making you the biggest returns in 20 years' time (Montag, 2019).

Dalio is also a big advocate of looking critically at market trends. If everyone wants to buy, what are the potential advantages of selling? If everyone wants to sell, what are the potential advantages of buying? If you follow your dollar-cost averaging strategy, you'll be steadily buying stock and accruing principal over the course of years. But if you want to experiment with buying or selling on other accounts or other assets, then knowing the psychology of the current market can help you make more informed decisions about what to do with your money.

The example that he uses is a great argument for the strength of the timeless investment strategy. After the market recovered from the 2008 recession, it entered the longest running bull market in stock market history, lasting even longer than the historical bull market after World War II. In those 10 years, the S&P 500 increased by 130%. If you had been following the timeless investment strategy during the 2008 recession, you would have been steadily buying stocks in your chosen company at your fixed dollar amount, ignoring the fluctuations of the market or the stock market panic around you.

Once the market recovered, you would have purchased a great deal of stock in your chosen company, which then would have gone on to earn you a 130% return over the course of the next 10 years. Had you decided to bail or change your strategy in the middle of the recession, you would undoubtedly have lost money. But because you're in it for the long haul, you're naturally insulated from these kinds of "crashes" and disasters that happen all the time. If you're well-versed in the stock market's history, then very little that happens in the future will be able to take you by surprise or push you off course (Montag, 2019).

By contrast, investors who didn't want to risk investing during the recession actually suffered for their caution. A diversified portfolio of 60% stocks and 40% bonds only returned about 8% over the last 10 years, while the interest rates on savings accounts have continued to shrink. Learning these kinds of historical "lessons" from the marketplace will help you to remain true to your own strategy. If you do decide to diversify, then these kinds of lessons will also help you to determine the best market conditions for branching out (Montag, 2019).

To use Dalio's words, don't judge what will be good in the near future by what's been good in the recent past. Whenever you're looking at the stock market, it should always be from the view of years or even decades, not from the view of days and months. Current trends and quarterly cycles are meaningless in the long-run. What's important to you is what will be happening in 10, 20, 30 years' time. And the best way to become more comfortable with the market's movements is to look at how it has changed over the past 10, 20, or 30 years.

Always focus on the long-term potential of any investment.

Finn, M. (n.d.). *turned on black iPhone 7* [photograph]. Retrieved from https://unsplash.com/photos/SgraLCyISWs

Sir John Templeton founded the Templeton Investment Group nearly 70 years ago. He formed this group based on 10 central tenets of investing. Today, the company still follows these investing rules, often referred to as the Templeton Maxims. These investment management principles have been applied by investors all over the world to great success, and are beloved by many because of their simplicity and straightforward logic.

### Invest for Real Returns

The ultimate goal of a long-term investor should always be maximum total real return after taxes. At the end of the day, that's what it's all about. The timeless investment strategy, Ray Dalio's 3-Step Formula, and any other long-term investment plan should be done with this mind. If you ever find yourself doubting or wavering in your investment plan, bring yourself back to this goal. Following your regular investment schedule is the surest way to ensure that you gain the highest possible return when it comes time for you to withdraw from your account in 40 years' time (Templeton, 2017).

### Keep an Open Mind

You are setting up your retirement account for the long-term, and that means that you want to choose assets that you're committed to. That being said, your commitment and discipline to regular investments in your chosen index fund will earn you the freedom and security to branch out as you desire. If you find yourself with extra money in the future and you want to experiment with different kinds of securities, you'll be able to do so while secure in the knowledge that your main retirement fund will be steadily growing year after year (Templeton, 2017).

### Never Follow the Crowd

Be very wary of marketplace trends. A reminder: if everyone is telling you that now is the time to buy, consider what might happen if you sell. If everyone is telling you that now is the time to sell, consider what might happen if you continue to buy. Blindly following "hot" tips or trendy behaviors rarely earns you any kind of reward. The most successful investors have built up their own rules and philosophies based on their own wisdom and experience. They don't change their habits or their mindset to blindly follow what's popular at the time. Stick to your investment schedule. Your dollar-cost averaging strategy will insulate you from dramatic changes in the market. And if you decide to branch out or you find yourself with money that you'd like to try investing in other securities, don't look to financial trends for advice. Don't do what's popular unless you can see the investment in front of you continuing to grow over the next 10 years (Templeton, 2017).

### Everything Changes

Bear markets are temporary. So are bull markets. No matter what the market looks like now, it will be different in a few months' time. Certain industries and securities may be popular with investors now, but that popularity could disappear in just a few years. When you're choosing companies or securities in which to invest, do so with the expectation that the market is going to change. Consider the possibility that the market will go down or jump up in just a few years' time. Will your investment still make sense if that happens? Consider the possibility that this asset, company, or security will no longer be popular in a few years' time? Will your investment continue to make sense after it loses its popularity? Will it still be making you money 20 years into the future? These are the important questions, the things to focus on when considering where to place your money.

### Avoid the Popular

In fact, following trends can sometimes jeopardize your investments. Too many investors can cause low stock prices to skyrocket, or valuable stocks to become worthless. If too many people flock to a certain asset or start selling all at once, then these behaviors can influence the future of the asset. The more you contribute to these trends, the more instability you introduce into the market. The more stable you are, on the other hand, the more stability to introduce to the market as a whole, protecting not only your own investments but the investments of others (Templeton, 2017).

### Learn from Your Mistakes

According to Templeton, "this time is different" are the four most expensive words an investor can utter. If you lose money on an investment, take the time to figure out why. Don't just look at external trends. Look closely at your own behavior. What could you have done differently to avoid incurring this loss? How is this going to change your own personal investing philosophy going forward? The great investors didn't invent their own personal philosophies based on their successes alone. For many of them, their wisdom comes just as much from their failures as it doesn't from the times that they were successful.

If you follow the timeless investment strategy, you're following a savings plan that's extremely low-risk. But if you decide to make personal adjustments to that strategy that ultimately don't work out, don't worry. Take a mental step back, learn from your mistake, and adjust your investment habits accordingly. Time is on your side. The earlier you start investing, the less your mistakes will cost you in the long-run (Templeton, 2017).

### Buy During Times of Pessimism

Bull markets begin as bear markets, and vice versa. The best time to buy is during a bear market, when stocks are low. Since your plan is one for the long-term, it doesn't matter what the market looks like right now. The important thing is that you get out there and start saving as soon as you can. So if the market is down right now, take heart. This is a great time for you to start buying. And if the market is up, wonderful! You're beginning your financial journey in a healthy market and a good economy. When the market inevitably goes down, continue to buy. Commit to your dollar-cost saving strategy. Don't deviate from your plan for one second. While everyone is fleeing the pessimistic market, you're doing the smartest thing you could possibly do by continuing to buy. When the market swings upward again, the jump in your fortunes will be enormous.

### Hunt for Value and Bargains

In a low-cost index fund like the S&P 500, it's difficult to go wrong. Therefore, when you're choosing which companies to invest in, take a look at what other investors are selling. Too many people place too much focus on outlook and trend, and not enough focus on value. Research the stocks that other investors seem eager to get rid of. Remember that even the best companies experience occasional dips in response to marketplace or economic trends. If you find that the company is stable, high-value, and has a bright future, take advantage of the blindness of other investors and start your investments while the buying is good (Templeton, 2017).

### Search Worldwide

The US is not the only financial marketplace on the globe. When you're first choosing your assets, if you stick with the S&P 500, you'll only be looking at American companies. But if you choose to diversify in the future, you may want to choose to invest in assets from other parts of the world. Diversification across multiple nations can actually be more secure than only investing in assets from your home country. The reason for this is that, while the global economy follows large-scale, general trends, each nation also follows its own individual trends. When the American market experiences a downturn, the UK's market may be experiencing a bump. When Canada is down, South Africa may be up. Diversifying across global markets can go a long way toward reducing risk by ensuring that, at any given time, at least one of your assets is on an upturn (Templeton, 2017).

### No One Knows Everything

Anyone who is trying to tell you that they have all the answers should be regarded with suspicion, including me! Don't take any financial advice wholesale. Apply what works for you in a way that makes sense for both your current financial situation and your goals for your financial future.

The facts and philosophies included in this chapter are far from the only ones out there. But as you begin researching and learning from different great investors, you'll start to see some common patterns in the advice that they give. For example, Jack Bogle is the creator of the Vanguard Group, another highly successful investment fund. Bogle, like Buffett, is another investor that's keen to spread his investment knowledge. His book *Enough: True Measures of Money, Business, and Life,* outlines seven life lessons that he learned from his time as an investor, and that any beginning investor can apply to their own mindsets in order to cultivate successful investment habits.

### Invest You Must

The biggest risk that investors face, mandates Bogle, is not short-term volatility, but the potential to not earn sufficient returns on their capital. The secret to insulating oneself against this risk? You guessed it - starting as early as possible. The more your capital accumulates, the more returns it will earn. Even the smartest, most disciplined investors with millions of dollars to spend aren't going to see the same kind of growth that the average investor in his 20s is going to see on the exact same asset (Tuchman, 2017).

### Time is Your Friend

I've said it a million times already in this book, but it can't be overstated. Even modest investments made early in life can grow to staggering returns over the course of a lifetime (Tuchman, 2017).

### Impulse is Your Enemy

As Bogle says so succinctly, avoid emotional responses. Don't react to the market out of fear - act according to logic. Make the choices that are going to provide you the most profit in the future. Don't make choices based on what you think might happen tomorrow, or next quarter.

### Basic Arithmetic Works

Bogle, like many other successful investors, insists on keeping investments as simple as possible. Keep investment expenses low. Avoid services that incur high-fees. When looking for a place to open an investment account, look for an index fund that's low-cost to avoid losing a significant portion of your returns to fees and hidden costs.

# Chapter 6: Myths, Traps, and Downright Lies

Don't jump on "trends" or "hot tips."

Distel, A. (n.d.-a). *person holding black iPhone displaying stock exchange* [photograph]. Retrieved from https://unsplash.com/photos/nGc5RT2HmF0

Investing is an industry filled with "facts" and "tips" that all-to-often turn out to be myths, traps, or even downright lies. For the new investor, it can be difficult to determine which-is-which. If you follow the timeless investment strategy and stay true to your investment schedule, that alone will protect you from falling for many of the more common traps. But many of the myths surrounding investing and the stock market are popularly considered to be truths. This chapter will debunk seven of these myths, so that you can begin your investing journey with your eyes wide open.

## Myth #1: Investing in Stocks is Like Gambling

For those who know nothing about stocks, this myth is too often accepted as being true. The fact that it's inherently unpredictable only serves to further prove to those who have never invested before that marketplace fluctuations are random, and that the stock market is therefore a dangerous way to save (Lincoln, 2019).

But as you know by now, the stock market is not a random game of chance. Unlike gambling, where the odds are intentionally stacked against you, the opposite is true of the stock market. Especially when investing over the long-term, the overwhelming trend of the market is upward, meaning that you're almost guaranteed to make money if you invest in companies with stable futures (Lincoln, 2019).

Since 1926, there has yet to be a period of 15 years in which the S&P 500 did not deliver a profit to its investors. It has also delivered a profit in 10% of 10-year periods after 1926, and 8% of 5-year periods. By contrast, how many Vegas casinos can promise a long-term return rate of between 86% and 100%?

But if this myth is so far-fetched, then why is this misconception so common? Because many first-time investors don't do that much research into the companies they choose to invest in. They either place all of their money into a "hot" stock that's been getting a lot of attention in financial headlines, or they place all of their money… anywhere, really.

Smart investors spread their investments out across multiple payments that are adjusted according to their income. This way, the income that you use to fuel your life is separate from the invested money riding the waves of the stock market. If you put everything you have into one stock, then your entire financial situation is at the mercy of the market's whims. So when the stock market goes down, you really do lose everything, because you have nothing to insulate your finances against it.

If you follow the timeless investment strategy, you will avoid making this and other common mistakes. Rather than losing it all on one reckless investment, you'll be making incremental payments over a lifetime toward a stock that's relatively stable. You'll adjust your payments according to your budget so that your investments don't compromise your financial security, and you'll have additional income and smart budgeting habits to insulate your personal finances against the natural fluctuations of the marketplace (Lincoln, 2019).

### Myth #2: It's Impossible to Beat the Market

This kind of myth plays into perceptions of the stock market as a kind of game that you "play" in order to "win" or "lose" money. But a smart investor doesn't need to "beat" the market because they understand that investment isn't a game (Lincoln, 2019).

When people say it's impossible to "beat" the market, what they're really trying to say is that it's impossible to make a significant amount of money by investing in stocks. Again, this is not true. It's hardly impossible to earn money investing in the stock market. It's a bit more difficult to make a significant amount of money. And it's more difficult still to hit your ideal financial targets.

The reason that many people feel that the market is "impossible" to beat is because they aren't investing in the long term. What's nearly impossible is making a significant amount of money from the stock market in a short amount of time.

But the timeless investment strategy follows an investing model known as "value" investing. This strategy understands that a disciplined investment strategy executed over the course of many years is not only possible to "beat" the market, it's actually extremely likely. Those who are trying complex strategies in order to make as much money as possible are often leaving something out, and that's time. The most powerful weapon against the market is time itself.

**Myth #3: Stock Market Investing is too Complex for the Average Investor**

Every investor makes mistakes that compromise some of their returns. But to follow the timeless investment strategy, all you have to do is buy into a low-cost passive index fund that tracks the S&P 500. If that's all you do, then you'll find yourself with hundreds of thousands of dollars in returns by the time you turn 65. Pretty simple, no?

As you get more comfortable investing, you can choose to branch out and start buying stock in less stable areas. But with time on your side, there's no need to do anything risky right now. You have the ability to watch the stock market fluctuate and practice making small, regular investments in your relatively fool-proof index fund. Investing can become complex, but it certainly doesn't have to be (Lincoln, 2019).

**Myth #4: You Can't Invest Unless You Have a Lot of Money**

The idea that investing is only for the rich and that you have to already have a significant amount of money before you can begin is probably the most toxic myth of all about the stock market. With a low-cost passive index fund, you can start investing with as little as $1 if you wish, and you can begin purchasing in many different stock portfolios with as little as $1,000 (Lincoln, 2019).

Since you're choosing a long-term investment strategy, you don't even have to worry about the price of the stocks you're buying. If you commit to a dollar-cost averaging strategy and make your regular investments, rain or shine, then the amount of stock you are able to buy in the company will average out to be quite a bit over time. And if you find a low-cost fund, you won't have to worry about brokerage fees eating away at your returns. The truth is that anyone can start investing. Small amounts of money invested now can grow into huge profits after they've been compounding for 40 years.

### Myth #5: Brokerage Trading Costs are Expensive and Eat Away at Profits

Not all brokerage fees are exorbitantly high. Yes, paying a $30 trading fee to buy and sell what only amounts to $100 worth of stock will certainly destroy your profit margin.

But the average brokerage fee is far less than $30, with most hovering between $5-$7. There are many reputable brokers that charge a flat rate, rather than incurring a fee with every trade. It's perfectly possible to find a broker who will charge you well under $10 per trade. Just keep your eyes open and your wits about you when opening new accounts or investing in new securities. $5 a trade will hardly eat away at your profits in the long-term, especially if you're investing a decent amount of money with each of your contributions.

### Myth #6: Stock Market Investing Will Take Too Much Time

If you wait to begin investing until you're in your 40s or 50s, then this myth might be true. But for everyone else, time is actually your friend. Time is what grows your invested capital into hundreds of thousands of dollars in profit.

But years spend accruing interest certainly do not have to be matched with hours of time a day spent managing your funds. Just 1-2 hours per *month* is all the management time you need after you set up your initial investment account and start automatically making your regular contributions. If the timeless investment strategy is enough for you, you could comfortably spend 1-2 hours per *year*, just to check on your earnings and make sure things are still operating smoothly. You can choose to spend as much or as little time as you wish managing your investments. Investing absolutely does not have to be a full-time job (Lincoln, 2019).

### Myth #7: You Don't Actually Lose Money on a Stock Unless You Sell It

This is an unfortunate misunderstanding of how your invested money fluctuates if you're investing for the long term. To some degree, it's true that you don't officially lose money until you "lock in" the trade by selling off the stock. If you wait for the stock to go back up, then you haven't actually lost any money. But it is important to remember that once your investment has declined, that's how much your share of the company is currently worth. If you choose to leave your money in that stock and wait for the value to increase once more, then the value of your money is simply riding the waves of the market's natural fluctuations. The passive nature of the strategy is what enables you to earn money in the long-run, even though it's weathering frequent ups and downs between your initial investment and the time you begin withdrawing (Lincoln, 2019).

I would not recommend selling stocks from your investment account until you're ready to start withdrawing. But if you want to expand your portfolio and start buying and selling with other stocks, just remember that you are continuously gaining and losing money as the value of your stocks rise and fall. While you can make reasonable predictions into the future, the only financial reality is what you have right now. So if you started with $10,000 and you currently have $9,000, you've lost money. But if you wait for your stocks to increase in value once again, then that $9,000 can quickly grow back up to $10,000 or even $15,000 once again. The longer your money sits, the more you will gain with each increase because of compound interest. That is what ultimately ensures that you make money over a long-term plan.

### Traps

Choose your investments wisely. Start with low-cost index funds.

Nowakowski, A. (n.d.-c). *man sitting in front of the MacBook pro* [photograph]. Retrieved from https://unsplash.com/photos/VkRq5w3asCA

The biggest trap any potential investor can fall into is choosing the wrong place to invest. The reason that I recommend low-cost index funds is that they're extremely stable. However, that also means that they're not very exciting. While you can earn a great deal of money in the long run, a passive index fund is rarely going to make you a lot of money in the short-term. It's for this reason that those who are trying to "beat" the market rarely invest their money in passive index funds. Those who want to insulate themselves fully against loss might make a great deal of money very quickly, but the frequent buying and selling of high-return stocks is a risky business. Because of the market's inherent unpredictability, this kind of behavior is a lot more like gambling than making regular contributions to an investment account that's attached to S&P 500 stock (Hamm, 2019).

The reason that trying to "beat" the market puts you in a gambler's mindset doesn't just have to do with marketplace volatility. When thinking about buying and selling high-return stocks, many people don't factor the cost of investment fees into their potential returns. While brokerage fees have a negligible effect on your long-term returns, they can definitely eat into any potential short-term gains (Hamm, 2019).

For example, imagine that you have $5,000 to invest. To buy the stocks you're interested in, you're going to have to pay a brokerage fee. Let's say you pay the average, $10. You're already down to $4,990 in stock value just from that one trade. When you decide to sell the stock, you're going to lose another $10 for that trade as well. So the stock you've purchased will have to "beat" the market by significantly more than $20 if you expect to make a reasonable return. If you're planning on investing in that stock for the next 40 years, this is hardly a concern. But if you're trying to ride the waves of the market to turn a quick profit on a "hot" stock, then your potential earnings are at the mercy of the market's movements.

It goes without saying that this kind of investing comes with a very high-risk potential. Let's return to the previous example. Let's say that 2% of stocks, regardless of when they are purchased, can reasonably be expected to match the market so well that you'll actually lose money to the $10 brokerage fee if you choose to sell. This means that, every time you purchase stock with the intention of selling for profit, there's a 52% chance that you will lose money. In other words, more than half the time, you're going to make more money by simply choosing another passive index fund to add to your overall retirement portfolio.

And while you can argue that this means there is a 48% chance that "hot" stock will earn you a profit, there's no guarantee that profit will be significant. This is why you want to be very careful when choosing which companies to invest in. Without doing your research, you could very well be blindsided when the "hot" stocks you just bought up are attached to a company that's announcing a huge quarterly loss. If you do your research, you'll be able to see that the company is in trouble. While everyone else is buying up that stock, you will continue making your regular contributions to your more stable investments.

Investment fees aren't the only extra costs that short-term investors (or those tempted to buy up some short-term, for-profit stocks) fail to enter into their calculations when trying to determine their potential for return. The other thing that everyone seems to forget about when it comes to the stock market is taxes (Hamm, 2019).

If you're investing in a retirement account that has built-in tax advantages, then this is something that you don't need to worry about. At least, not if you're investing that money responsibly. Considering how much you're practically guaranteed to make if you make regular contributions to boring, passive index funds, it's extremely irresponsible to waste those savings on risky purchases or erratic buying and selling.

In a normal, taxable account, you have to pay taxes on all of your gains and losses; if you're trading all the time, then your gains will be considered short-term gains, which are taxed at a higher rate. Sitting for years on an index fund, on the other hand, means that, when it comes time to withdraw, the only taxes you'll be responsible for are long-term capital gains taxes, which are much lower (Hamm, 2019).

But perhaps the biggest problem with the "beat the market" mindset is your own psychology. Humans are hard-wired to react emotionally to stressful situations, and sudden jumps or dips in price definitely count as a stressful situation if you're trying to turn a quick profit on a risky investment. Buying low and selling high are sensible concepts on paper, but even the most stoic investor can find it difficult to hold on to stocks that are falling in price or to resist buying the rapidly climbing, "hot" stock to take advantage of what seems like a good opportunity. Making regular payments on a passive index fund protects you from any of these emotional highs and lows. If you automate your regular contributions, you don't need to look at the stock market at all.

A big investment trap is the idea that, with enough research, you'll be able to predict the market, and therefore make big profits buying and selling based on this knowledge. But again, there are a number of flaws with this logic. First and foremost, past performance is never indicative of future returns. The price history of the stock has everything to do with the economic and psychological realities of the marketplace at the time, and can tell you nothing about how that stock is expected to do in the future. The prices of individual stocks are constantly rising and falling. The only kind of research that can give you any kind of indicator as to how well a stock is going to perform on the market is researching the *company*, and what kind of future it has a business.

It won't take long to determine which companies are stable enough for you to invest in for the long term. But if you're trying to turn a quick profit and "beat" marketplace fluctuations, then the kind of research you'd have to do into a company in order to predict its stock performance on the market would be extensive indeed. To even have a chance of accurately predicting how a company's stock is going to perform, you'd have to read through all of the company's SEC filings and annual reports. It's not enough to know what the company does and how it operates. You'll have to have an intimate understanding of how the company is currently doing as a business, how trustworthy its upper management staff is, and how the sector in which the company currently operates is doing financially (Hamm, 2019).

Doing all of that research into a company is going to take time. A lot of time. Let's say you're willing to spend 20 hours a week doing homework on a "hot" company to see if its stock is going to continue to climb for the foreseeable future. This may give you enough of a competitive edge to reliably beat the market by a percent or two. So to even earn minimum wage on the time you're putting in, you'd have to invest a great deal of money in order to make that 1% or 2% gain something that could reasonably compensate you for the time you're putting in. So unless you have six or seven figures worth of investment money to spend, "researching" the market is never going to be worth in returns the amount of time you spend studying in order to have a truly competitive understanding of market trends (Hamm, 2019).

And even if you did put 20 hours a week into studying the market, you'd still be perpetually behind the curve when it comes to working with updated information. You're not someone who works in the company that you're researching, nor are you an institutional investor. So when a company makes a decision or is preparing to release some pertinent financial information about its assets, there are many people who are going to know that information before you do. Investment firms pay entire staffs of full-time people to do the same research that you're doing for free. This means that they're going to be able to react to market trends much faster than you can, and often on more reliable streams of information. If a company is in trouble, you're still going to be the last to know, even if you're dedicating 20 hours a week to researching their assets. More often than not, this will mean that the value of the stock will fall before you ever have a chance to sell. Even if you can predict the coming downturn, you won't get the information fast enough to act on it.

If you're willing to do this kind of study full-time, then you might be able to tout yourself as an accurate marketplace predictor. But if you don't want your investment to eat up hours of your time, it's best to find a historically strong company that you can trust will still be making money in 20 years' time (Hamm, 2019).

So if the idea of "beating" the market is so risky and flawed, why do so many people think they can do it? This kind of thinking is often predicated on stories of investment giants of the past who managed to "beat" the market year after year on the skill of their investing savvy alone. But this kind of mythologizing is also a kind of psychological trap, for the simple reason that many of these investing giants did what they did in a very different era.

Back in the 1970s and 80s, there was far less computer-based trading, and far less sophisticated programs for market analytics. Hedge funds and high-frequency trading didn't exist back then, either. So in 1975, it may have been possible to gain a real competitive edge on the market with 20 hours a week of dedicated study and a sizable savings with which to play. But those days are done. Today, it would be nearly impossible to learn enough, and fast enough, to earn enough to make your time worth it (Hamm, 2019).

### What You Don't Know CAN Hurt You

As you begin your investment journey, there are some important words to keep an eye out for. While many of these concepts aren't inherently profit killers, they are often presented in a way that makes them look more beneficial than they really are. If you see any of these words, pay careful attention and make sure that you do your research before making any kind of investment.

### ETFs

Otherwise known as exchange-traded funds. Essentially, an ETF is an investment fund in which an investor can buy and sell shares. ETFs can hold any kind of asset (stocks, bonds, or commodities) whose values fluctuate with the market. They have high liquidity and usually track an index. This is by far the most common exchange-trade product on the market, as it puts all of your assets into one account and makes day-trading extremely simple. If you choose an ETF for your investment fund, however, there are a few things to remember. The first is that ETFs, unlike retirement accounts, are fully taxable. The second thing is that, while ETFs do tend to have lower fees than other kinds of accounts, they often come with hidden fees, so make sure you're reading the fine print before you purchase a fund (Robbins Research International, Inc., 2019).

### Expense Ratio

This is the total expense of a stock or fund's operating expenses divided by the average dollar value of its assets under management. In other words, what is it costing the investment firm to operate the fund? For example, a 1% expense ratio would mean that 1% of the fund's total assets are being used to cover the fund's expenses. This sounds harmless, yes? But the thing to remember is that this is a *fee*. That 1% is going to come from your earnings. While 1% is a standard expense ratio for domestic stock funds, index funds often come with much lower ratios (Robbins Research International, Inc., 2019).

### Sales Charge

This is the commission paid to a broker or financial advisor by the investor for purchasing mutual funds on the investor's behalf. This can vary greatly, and smaller commissions aren't always better. Brokers take the size of their commissions into account when determining whether or not to sell the fund. Though brokers who trade for "free" with commission may sound attractive, this is why it's typically better to find someone who will trade for a flat rate per transaction (Robbins Research International, Inc., 2019).

### No Load

A no-load mutual fund is sold without a commission or a sales charge. This means that 100% of the investor's money remains in the investor's account, without percentages being taken out before or after transactions to pay commission fees. However, a no-load fund still charges a management fee (that's the expense ratio) and often charges other fees as well. So while they can sometimes be advertised as "free," they aren't.

### Exchange Fee

Some mutual funds charge investors when they transfer from one fund to another within the same "family" of funds. This is another fee to be on the watch for, and one that you will avoid if you can choose a fund that you plan on sticking with for the long-haul.

### Cash Drag

This is often touted in investment literature as a good thing, but be careful. This is the uninvested cash that a fund manager sets aside, often with the purpose of handling withdrawals from the fund. However, since this portion of the fund is not invested, its value won't fluctuate with the market. This means that it can't grow, and that it doesn't accrue interest, which is the real money-maker. Even worse, you're often expected to pay fees on this portion of the fund, especially when it's time to withdraw.

### Structured Notes

This is essentially a loan agreement with a bank, in which the bank agrees to hold your money for a specified number of years. At the end of this period, the bank will issue you a note, 100% of your money back, as well as a percentage of the upside of the market or index. This is an extremely safe investment that's almost guaranteed to make you money, but unlike the timeless investment strategy, it won't make you very much. In addition, these kinds of agreements almost always come with high and hidden fees, which will further eat into whatever your money earns while it's being stored for you. If you do decide to do this, consider going through a fee-based fiduciary advisor. This kind of advisor legally can't charge you any fees, and can act as a liaison between you and the bank to help you avoid any fees that aren't necessary (Robbins Research International, Inc., 2019).

### 4% Rule

This is a bit of financial advice that applies to investors after it's time for them to withdraw from their retirement account. This rule suggests that, rather than withdrawing the entire sum, investors withdraw just 4% of their earnings annually, allowing the rest to continue to grow even while they're in retirement. The only problem with this rule, of course, is that 4% is quite a conservative number. If you start investing now, you may have a retirement account big enough to live on just 4% a year when it's time to retire. But for most people, even those who have invested a great deal over the course of years, this number just isn't realistic (Robbins Research International, Inc., 2019).

### High Frequency Trading

Often shortened to HFT, this trading method is basically what it sounds like. These firms use powerful computers and complex algorithms to process incredibly high numbers of orders at dizzyingly fast speeds. These traders move in and out of trade within seconds, often with the intention of making less than a cent in profit with each trade. This kind of trading is for investment firms and companies powered by entire staffs of full-time people. This kind of trading is not for a single person looking to secure their financial future.

### Momentum Trading

In this strategy, traders focus on stocks that are moving at a significant rate in one direction or another at a high volume, and attempt to make a profit from this sudden wave in momentum. This kind of trading is speculative, extremely high risk, and extremely high energy. Momentum traders watch the market for hours every day looking for trends, and will often only hold their position for a few minutes or hours, just enough to turn a profit before selling at the last minute. This kind of trading might make you a small profit in the short term, but it will never earn you anywhere near what you can make as a long-term investor.

### Dollar-Cost Averaging

Sometimes called the "constant dollar plan," this strategy is the foundation of the timeless investment strategy. I include it here, however, because there are a few key ways in which this strategy is often misused by investors. The key to this strategy's success is consistency, both in dollar amount and in time. If you commit to making a contribution to your investment every week, don't miss a week. If you commit to contributing every month, make sure it happens every single month, 12 months a year. If you only contribute to your investment account when you feel like it or when you happen to have extra money, the principal that you've already invested will continue to grow. But less you have in your account, the more you lose in compound interest over time. This is why the dollar amount is important, too.

If you lower your payments in bad markets and increase them during bull markets, you're actually doing yourself a disservice. It can't be stressed enough that the benefit of sticking to the same regular contribution amount is that it evens out your risk of loss. In low markets, you'll be able to purchase more stocks with the same amount of money. And in high markets, not only will you make a profit on those extra stocks, but you'll be continuing to purchase valuable stocks in a good market. This strategy protects you in both good markets and bad, but only if it's followed with care and strict regularity (Robbins Research International, Inc., 2019).

### Poison Pills

Sometimes referred to as a "shareholder rights plan," this is a strategy that companies employ to discourage a hostile takeover during a high market. To make stocks less attractive to potential buyers, the company will intentionally lower the value of its stocks. This both decreases buyer interest in the company and essentially gives current shareholders a discount on their shares, because the lowering in value doesn't reflect the true financial situation of the company. Once the threat of a hostile takeover has passed, the company will increase the value of its stocks once again. This is yet another reason why you can't use stock value or market trends to determine how well a company is doing or what kinds of investing decisions you should make. If you responded to this kind of decrease in value by selling your stock in order to avoid a loss, then you'd be losing money in the long-run. There's a lot more going on behind the market's rising and falling than meets the eye. This is why it's much simpler and more profitable to stick with one or two reliable companies and just let your money grow over time (Robbins Research International, Inc., 2019).

### Taxes

The bottom line is, you'll have to pay them. One way or another, whatever you earn through your investments is going to be taxed; whether it's by the federal government, the state, social security, Medicare, or all of the above. Any investment strategy that promises to show you how to "avoid" paying taxes is misleading you. The smart investor understands that taxes are inevitable, and doesn't try to avoid them altogether. Instead, the trick is to lower the amount you're going to be taxed as much as possible (Robbins Research International, Inc., 2019)

The timeless investment strategy is inherently a low-tax strategy because it automatically qualifies you for long-term gain taxes, which are much lower than short-term gain taxes. If you let your money sit in a retirement account for years before withdrawing, then the amount you'll be taxed on your earnings is negligible compared to the percentages you'd be paying out if you were constantly buying and selling for profit. If you choose to invest your money in a retirement account, especially a 401(k), then you will also lower your tax account through the tax protections that come with the account (Robbins Research International, Inc., 2019).

# Chapter 7: Everything You Need to Start Making Money Today

$1 invested, grows and grows - start small, if you need to.

Brand, N. (n.d.). *1 US dollar banknote* [photograph]. Retrieved from https://unsplash.com/photos/8fDhgAN5zG0

Now you know what the timeless investment strategy is all about. You understand how the market works, what you look for when choosing where to invest your money, and red flags to avoid. Now it's time for you to get started.

The very first step is for you to choose a broker or platform through which you can purchase your stocks. There are a number of reputable places for you to do this, but there are a few places where I've seen people consistently find success (Reinkensmeyer, 2020).

### TD Ameritrade

TD Ameritrade offers investors an excellent package, including $0 trades and an easy-to-use online trading platform. The platform also offers investors access to market research, industry-leading education geared toward first-time investors, and very reliable customer service (Reinkensmeyer, 2020).

TD Ameritrade's main online trading platform is a program called thinkorswim. This platform manages to be extremely user-friendly and highly sophisticated at the same time. Perhaps the best feature of all is the mobile app, which allows you to manage your investments no matter where you are in the world.

This is also an excellent trading space for beginning investors. TD Ameritrade is noted for the amount and quality of education materials that it offers its investors, including well over 200 videos in which industry professionals discuss every investment topic you can possibly think of. The learning center is structured in a game-like format, with features that track your progress the more you learn and testing your knowledge with quizzes at the end of each course.

TD Ameritrade also offers investors access to its own TV network and trader magazine, making it extremely easy for investors to do research and keep up with the market, if they wish to. They also offer investors access to social media data, which they accrue via proprietary data that tracks millions of tweets.

Finally, TD Ameritrade seems to be the most forward-thinking broker in terms of technology. It's the only trading platform that you can connect to through Twitter, Facebook, Apple Chat, and Alexa, making it one of the most easily accessible trading platforms currently available to investors (Reinkensmeyer, 2020).

*TD Ameritrade's Features At a Glance (Reinkensmeyer, 2020):*

Minimum Deposit - $0

Stock Trades - $0 per trade

Option Trades - $0+$0.65 per contract

Commission-Free ETFs - all

Trading Platform - thinkorswim

## Fidelity

Fidelity is another online broker that's value driven, offering $0 stock trades, access to professional research, high-quality trading tools, a sophisticated mobile app, and excellent retirement services. Fidelity currently serves over 30 million customers, and is perhaps the best trading platform out there for the everyday investor that's not affiliated with a firm or company.

Fidelity also offers an impressive wealth of investment research to its investors. Its 16 equity research reports and in-house market analysis are both easily accessible and of an extremely high quality. Fidelity also offers a number of networking resources where investors can share their own personal experiences and learn from those who are more successful in the field.

This experience-focused approach to research also makes Fidelity an excellent choice for beginning investors. Tied only with TD Ameritrade, Fidelity offers more than most trading platforms in terms of user-friendly, high-quality research tools. They also provide investors access to an education center that is both easy to use and connects first-time investors with materials written by some of the most successful people in the industry.

Fidelity also offers investors a very sophisticated mobile app. Not only is it easy to use, but it provides investors with mobile access to educational materials and trading tools, making it very easy to manage your money on the go.

*Fidelity's Features At a Glance:*

Minimum Deposit - $0

Stock Trades - $0 per trade (Reinkensmeyer, 2020)

Option Trades - $0.65 per trade (Reinkensmeyer, 2020)

Commission-Free ETFs - all

Trading Platform - Active Trader Pro

### Charles Schwab

Charles Schwab is one of the oldest and most reliable brokerages in the business, having been in operation since 1975. This low-cost platform also offers investors $0 stock trades, access to high quality stock research, education for beginning investors, high quality trade tools, and access to professional planning for the future.

Every week, Schwab's team of 26 industry experts post articles via Charles Schwab's educational blog called Schwab Insights. They also offer a number of high-quality retirement services, including Schwab Intelligent Portfolios, a robo-advisor, and Schwab Intelligent Portfolios Premium, a human advisor, to go over your retirement options and answer any questions you may have.

*Charles Schwab's Features At a Glance:*

Minimum Deposit - $0

Stock Trades - $0 per trade

Option Trades - $0.65 per contract

Commission-Free ETFs - all

Trading Platform - StreetSmart Edge

### E*Trade

E*Trade was one of the first online trading platforms available in the market, going online in 1982. E*Trade offers $0 stock trades, not one, but two excellent mobile apps, and the Power E*Trade Platform which offers a number of great features to options traders.

Power E*Trade is perhaps one of the best online trading platforms available to investors. It's much better for options trading, but it's still a decent platform for stock traders as well.

E*Trade also offers more mobile options than many other online traders. Both of its mobile apps are remarkably easy to use, and offer more features than most of the mobile apps offered by other trading platforms (Reinkensmeyer, 2020).

*E*Trade Features At a Glance (Reinkensmeyer, 2020):*

Minimum Deposit - $0

Stock Trades - $0 per trade

Option Trades - $0.65 per contract

Commission-Free ETFs - all

Trading Platform - Power E*Trade

### Interactive Brokers

Interactive Brokers is a far better platform for professionals, but its low-cost offerings are still decent for casual investors. Through its Trader Workstation Platform, it also offers investors very easy access to an extensive array of tradable securities.

Interactive Brokers also offers its investors a staggering 63 different order types, more than any other trading platform by a long-shot. It's also known throughout the industry for its consistently low margin rates.

Interactive Brokers also does not accept payment for order flow, which keeps it low-cost and almost guarantees that investors won't incur any hidden or unnecessary exchange fees. And for those who are looking to expand into the global market, Interactive Brokers enables its investors to trade in 26 countries across 135 market centers.

*Interactive Brokers' Features At a Glance:*

Minimum Deposit = $0

Stock Trades - $0-$0.005 per share

Option Trades - $0-$0.65 per contract

Commission-Free ETFs - all or 48, depending

Trading Platform - Trader Workstation

### Merrill Edge

Backed by Bank of America, Merrill Edge offers $0 on stock trades and is perhaps the safest place for ETF trades. And if you're a Bank of America customer, you stand to earn some pretty significant rewards benefits if you choose to open an investment account with Merrill Edge (Reinkensmeyer, 2020).

You don't have to be a Bank of America customer to trade with Merrill Edge, but it's a far more profitable enterprise if you are. Their preferred rewards programs gives investors all kinds of perks for reaching certain account balances, which is a powerful motivator to continue investing and saving (Reinkensmeyer, 2020).

It also offers an impressive array of research portfolios, categorized and presented to investors via the Stock Story, Fund Story, and Portfolio Story. They also include full ESG reports that are easily available for any investor. But where Merrill Edge truly earns the gold star is in customer service, which is available in minutes 24/7.

*Merrill Edge's Features At a Glance:*

Minimum Deposit - $0

Stock Trades - $0 per trade

Option Trades - $0.65 per contract

Commission-Free ETFs - all

Trading Platform - Merrill Edge MarketPro

## TradeStation

TradeStation is relatively new on the scene, but it's online trading platform is easily one of the best in the industry. TradeStation also offers its investors $0 stock and ETF trades.

The award-winning, desktop-based platform is robust and equipped with a number of sophisticated investment tools that are easy to use. Perhaps the only platform that is as comprehensive and user-friendly is TD Ameritrade's thinkorswim platform.

Its mobile app also comes with a number of relatively unique features, including the ability to monitor multiple watch lists, set price alerts, analyze stock charts, and even place trades. The app is easy and user-friendly, making it a great option for beginner or casual traders, but its array of features also makes it a good option for more experienced investors.

*TradeStation's Features At a Glance:*

Minimum Deposit - $0

Stock Trades - $0 per trade (Reinkensmeyer, 2020)

Option Trades - $0.50 per contract (Reinkensmeyer, 2020)

Commission-Free ETFs - all

Trading Platform - TradeStation 10

### More Platforms

While the platforms already reviewed in this chapter are some of the biggest and most reputable in the industry, they are far from the only places where you as a beginning investor can have a good investment experience. Smaller platforms don't always offer you the same kinds of resources, but they can sometimes offer you a more personal experience. If you stick to the timeless investment strategy without branching out too far, then the personalized experiences that these smaller brokers offer might even be preferable to the colder, corporate offerings of high-powered platforms.

*Ally Invest*

This low-cost broker provides $0 stock and ETF trades. It's online platform and account management tools make it a very easy platform to use, and it offers some perks to current Ally Bank customers.

*Firstrade*

This broker provides $0 stock, ETF, and options trades and a very easy-to-use platform. Where Firstrade stands out is its full Chinese-language services, for those who may be more comfortable trading in Mandarin. It also offers a decent offering of industry research and a variety of trading tools, making it a good choice for beginning investors.

*Chase You Invest Trade*

This is a very convenient trading option for Chase Bank customers. The site is reliable and easy-to-use, but its features are far more profitable for those who already have a bank account open with Chase (Reinkensmeyer, 2020).

*SogoTrade*

This is another online broker that offers a great deal of support to Chinese-speaking customers. It charges $4.88 in base commissions, which makes it quite a pricey option compared to other brokers. However, it does offer five different platforms for both stocks and options traders. If you're planning to stick to the timeless investment strategy, this platform may not be worth it. But if you're looking to expand your portfolio over time and are interested in the Chinese market specifically, it may be worth a look (Reinkensmeyer, 2020).

### The Secret to Generational Wealth

You don't have to earn a lot in order to retire a lot. You don't even have to invest a lot in order to retire with a lot. Commitment, discipline, and good financial habits are what give you the true edge when it comes to financial security. You may be looking around you and thinking that people your age who grew up with wealth have the competitive edge, but this isn't necessarily true. If you start investing now, then you, with your minimum-wage job and your mountain of student debt, will be miles ahead of your wealthy friends who don't start investing until later in life, or who even never decide to reinvest their wealth at all.

In the words of Tony Robbins, ending up rich starts with paying yourself first. Every time you save or invest, you can think of that as income. It's your current self-paying your future self, so that you don't have to work or worry about money when you're in your 60s and 70s (Elkins, 2019).

The idea that wealth belongs only to the wealthy is a toxic idea, one that stops too many average people from earning the money that they deserve by investing. The size of your salary is nothing compared to the amount of time your money spends compounding or the regularity with which you make your minuscule contributions. As we've seen over and over again, there is no investment contribution that is too small. To illustrate the point, let's look at a UPS driver named Theodore Johnson (Elkins, 2019). Early into his career, a mentor advised him to save and invest 20% of every paycheck. At first, he protested. UPS drivers don't make very much money to begin with. How was he supposed to live on 20% less income? Furthermore, 20% of a UPS driver's monthly income isn't very much. How could that possibly grow into a retirement fund?

Fortunately for Johnson, he eventually followed his mentor's advice. Though it was difficult at first, he eventually adjusted his lifestyle and learned to live on 20% less than he was making. And when it came time to retire, he found himself with $700,000 in company stock; and that was in 1952 - in today's dollars that's $6.8 million. He continued to invest, and eventually built his fortune of more than $70 million. The meager 20% of his humble salary had grown into a fortune through years of discipline and compound interest.

To be fair, Johnson did make a few other smart investments along the way. He bought as much as he could of the company stock, and his successful career allowed him to make bigger and bigger investment contributions throughout his life. Though he started as a humble driver earning minimum wage, by the time he retired, he had climbed the company ladder to vice president for industrial relations. His yearly salary at the time he retired was $14,000, which today would be more than $130,000. But good financial habits are part of the big picture, and the point stands that even the humblest of savings can grow into a fortune.

The secret is to start early and contribute regularly. Even if you can only spare a tiny percentage of your income to a retirement account, it's much better to start small than to not start at all. Even if you wait to open an investment account until you're established in a career, the high contributions you make will pale in comparison to interest that your tiny payments could have been collecting while you were working your way up the corporate ladder (Elkins, 2019).

The most successful way to make regular investment contributions is to have the funds withdrawn automatically from your checking account every week or month. That way, you don't have to remind yourself to do it, or get away with "forgetting" to make your contributions. You will also be more disciplined to keep that money in your account, as an automatic withdrawal will overdraft your account if you've spent that money elsewhere. For example, imagine that you are making $50,000 per year. Investing 10 percent of that income would mean investing $5,000 a year. If you try to invest that money all at once, it will feel like a huge sum. But if you spread that out over 12 monthly payments, that $5,000 shrinks to $417 a month (plus the interest compounded on each of those payments).

If you make a regular weekly payment, that investment shrinks down to $105 per week. Small, frequent payments make you more money in interest, but more importantly, they're easier to commit to. Make your initial payments as small as necessary in order to make them seem doable. It's far better to regularly invest $10 a week than it is to invest $5,000 all at once, blow your budget, and decide that investing is a scam (Elkins, 2019).

But perhaps the most important thing to remember about investing is that you can always increase your contributions. In your 20s, you have nothing. That's how most Americans start out. But the average household income in the United States is $61,372, which means that you're unlikely to remain that way. A stable career and a higher salary is in your future. When you start earning more money, you can make larger contributions. For now, your small contributions will get the snowball rolling and make your future contributions count for even more than they would normally.

NerdWallet provides a testament to the power of compound interest, as well as the power of starting early. Their example person opens an investment account at age 22. They start with zero dollars invested. Their personal financial goal is to have $2 million in savings when they retire. NerdWallet's calculator assumes an average annual gain of 6% on this person's investments. This number is actually a bit lower than the average annual return of the S&P

500, so it's a reasonable example of what's possible for you if you choose to follow the timeless investment strategy (Elkins, 2019).

According to NerdWallet's calculator, $167 a week invested over 20 years is enough to earn you $2 million (at least) by the time you're 65. While this is going to feel like a huge sum in the beginning when your yearly income is $40,000 or less, it will get easier and easier as you start to make more money in the future. The most important thing to remember about investing is that the hardest part is in the beginning. Over time, it gets exponentially easier to save. But the longer you wait, the harder it will be for you to catch up to the people who started saving 10 years before you. Using this same model, a 30-year-old would have to put a way more than double that amount every week to earn the same amount of money (Elkins, 2019).

The secret to wealth is that it's not about how much money you have, or even about how much money you make. It's about how much money you spend. Athletes and celebrities that make millions of dollars a year still manage to find themselves bankrupt and assetless. No matter how much money you're making, if you spend more than you earn, then you're poor.

Is it easier to save with more money? Of course. But it's not impossible to save with a little money, and the secret is that the more you save, the more money you have. The more money you have, the easier it is to save. And if you're putting your savings into an investment account, then you are contributing to a beneficial cycle of wealth that will continue to grow over the course of your lifetime.

The secret to wealth is saving your money in ways that will earn you the most returns over time. And the secret to generation wealth is that inheritances are much more easily spent than they are earned. The children of billionaires don't necessarily grow up to become billionaires themselves. While it might seem like an advantage to be born into money, there's a big difference between having a wealthy family and being wealthy yourself. Anyone can earn enough money through investing to provide them with complete security and freedom when they retire, no matter where they come from or how much money they began their investment trajectory with. At age 65, it won't matter how much money you started with. You'll come out on top because you've been investing and using your money wisely throughout your life. Those that started out with an edge will find that edge quickly disappear if they don't learn to manage their own money.

## A Step-by-Step Guide to Get You Started On Your Investment Journey

### Step #1: Understand that it's Better to "Be" the Market than Beat the Market

Once you've found an online broker that will support your financial goals, find two or three S&P 500 companies that you can guarantee will still be in existence 40 years from now. You can expand, experiment, and diversify later in life when you have the extra funds. But this account isn't about getting rich quick. It's not even about getting rich soon. This is about securing your financial future. No matter what you make or how you live from now until age 65, this account is about guaranteeing that, when the time comes, you and your family will be taken care of. Get all thoughts of "beating" and "playing" the market out of your head. You're in it for the long haul. You don't have to beat the market - you are the market (O'Shea, 2020).

### Step #2: Set Aside a Cash Cushion of X months

If at all possible, siphon off a big chunk of cash that you can break down over the course of several months. This will get you comfortably started on your investment journey without having too much of an impact on your current budget. Whether it's a $1,000 tax return or a $500 Christmas check from Grandma, take any extra money you have and invest it. Once that money runs its course, you'll be on a regular investment schedule and you'll be in the right mindset for when that money starts coming out of your monthly income.

An alternative way to use this approach is to match the contributions that come from your cash cushion with money from your income. So for example, imagine that your regular investment amount is going to be $100 a month. If you spread your $1,000 income tax out at that rate, it'll last 10 months. But for the next ten months, don't just rely on the income tax to make your investment payments. Invest the designated $100 a week from your income, and then invest an additional $100 a week from the tax return. This will give your investment account a little bit of a head start, a little bit of extra principal that will make you thousands of dollars in compound interest throughout the rest of your life (O'Shea, 2020).

### Step #3: Buy a Low-Cost Index Fund Every Month and Automate the Process

You'd done your budget. You have the cash. You've created an account with an online broker. Now it's time to start making the payments. Whether you make your regular contributions every month or every week, make sure that you automate the process to keep yourself on track (O'Shea, 2020).

### Step #4: Stay the Course

It's hard to stay disciplined. Your account isn't growing very fast. The market is experiencing a downturn. These and other thoughts will flow through your head, especially over the course of the first few years. Let those thoughts come in, and then let them go right back out (O'Shea, 2020).

### Step #5: Stay the Course

Making an average return of 7-10% every year on your investments is easy, as long as you follow this critical and important step. At rate of return, you'll see your money double after 10 years' time, and double again before you stop making regular contributions. But too many people make it this far only to pull out because of an emotionally-based decision. Perhaps there will be another recession. Perhaps a friend or an article you read online has convinced you to put your money in a riskier asset. Do everything you can to resist these temptations along the way. Make your regular contributions to your retirement account, no matter how you feel, no matter what you read or hear or what's going on in the news.

Stay the course, through thick and thin, and you will find yourself enjoying an unprecedented amount of wealth when it comes time to withdraw.

# Conclusion: A New Beginning

Set your budget for saving, and start investing - today!

Distel, A. (n.d.-c). *turned-on android smartphone* [photograph]. Retrieved from https://unsplash.com/photos/pfmKvWLDGoc

You've done it. You've made up a budget. You know what your financial goals are, and how much money you'll need to invest within a certain number of years in order to reach those goals. You've determined a reasonable contribution amount to invest out of every paycheck. You've found a broker with which to open an investment account. You've found a low-cost index fund that follows the S&P 500. You know which two or three companies you'd like to invest in. Now all you have to do…is do it.

Don't wait for one more second. Don't wait for tomorrow, or next week, or this coming weekend. Do it now. Every day that you wait to invest is a potential loss of hundreds of dollars in accrued interest on payments that you could have been making for months now. Don't allow anyone to talk you out of your plan or convince you that you aren't making enough right now to invest. Don't allow your own fears or insecurities to stop you. If you don't want to give up that much of your paycheck, just start by investing $1 a week.

At this point, you've seen over and over again how much a $1 investment can grow in 5, 10, or even 15 years. Now it's time to think about how much money you'll have in 30, 40, 50, or even 60 years from now. It may seem far in the future, but it will come up faster than you think. What are you going to do with your earnings?

If you had millions of dollars to play with right now, how would you spend it? Would you donate to a cause that you believe in? Start a business? Give it to your family? These don't have to be fantasies or dreams. If you see something wrong with the world, commit yourself to saving as much money as you can to finally be able to make a real difference. If you want to insulate future generations from the financial hardships that you are facing now, thinking about how much money you want to give to your children or grandchildren. Every time you make an investment, let your dreams grow bigger. The money that you're investing isn't a dream, nor are the numbers that you see when you check your investment account every year.

In the words of Tony Robbins, the transition from growing to giving is a spiritual one, one that makes the difference between a world that's dark and cynical and a world that's safe and beautiful. The money that you're earning can represent whatever you want. Retirement doesn't have to be all luxury cruises and expensive vacations if you don't want it to be. Whatever difference you want to make in the world, you can use that money to translate your dreams into reality. Every time you invest, you're giving yourself the opportunity to give back to the world in a big way when you have years of wisdom, maturity, and experience to compliment the money that you'll have saved over time.

At this point, you now have all the tools that you need to set yourself up with an investment strategy that is nearly iron-clad. If you have any questions along the way, you can easily come back to one of the chapters in this book for guidance or clarification. Though your brain is probably swimming with information, the most important takeaway is that investing doesn't have to be complex. It doesn't have to be hard. It doesn't have to be difficult.

Once you take the first step, you'll know what I'm talking about. The concepts that seem complex on paper are refreshingly simple in real life. If you follow the guidance outlined in this book, you can rest assured that you are making a smart and sensible financial choice, one that is predicated on countless examples.

This strategy is based on the teachings and experience of some of the most successful people in the world today. There are hundreds of examples of people who have followed this strategy and found themselves with more money than they ever dreamed possible when it came time to retire. You do not have to be resigned to a future fraught with financial insecurity. People lose money playing the stock market all the time, but consider this book as a kind of map or compass, steering you through safe and sensible waters. Over time, you'll watch other people around you make mistakes, but if you stay the course, you'll find yourself reaching your goals with ease.

## Free Bonus

You need to stop what you're reading right now. Hey, this sounds counterintuitive isn't it? Well, the reason is simple. I have a free bonus set up for you. The problem is this: we forget 90% of everything that we read after 7 days. Crazy fact, right? Here's the solution: I've created a printable, 1-page pdf summary for you… in regards to this book.

All you have to do now is visit billgrand.com/hello. Once you visit billgrand.com/hello, it will be intuitive. Enjoy & thank you!

# References


Edwards, C. (2016, January 22). Warren Buffett's Best Money Advice. https://www.workandmoney.com/s/warren-buffetts-best-money-advice-72f4feae75644d44

Elkins, K. (2019, January 5). Tony Robbins: Here's how to retire rich on a normal person's income. https://www.cnbc.com/2019/01/04/tony-robbins-heres-how-to-retire-rich-on-a-normal-persons-income.html

Elkins, K. (2020, February 4). This simple formula tells you how long it will take for your money to double—while you sit back and relax. https://www.cnbc.com/2020/01/28/what-the-rule-of-72-is-and-how-it-works.html

Fidelity Viewpoints. (2020a, March 19). Six habits of successful investors | Fidelity. https://www.fidelity.com/viewpoints/investing-ideas/six-habits-successful-investors

Friedberg, B. (2020, March 31). Money Saving Tips From Warren Buffett. https://barbarafriedbergpersonalfinance.com/saving-money-advice-warren-buffett/

Hamm, T. (2019, October 29). Why 'Beating the Stock Market' Is a Lie. https://www.thesimpledollar.com/investing/stocks/why-beating-the-stock-market-is-a-lie/

Housel, M. (2018, June 1). The Psychology of Money. https://www.collaborativefund.com/blog/the-psychology-of-money/

Kunsman, T. (2020, April 14). 35 Investing Terms: The Key Words Beginners Need to Know First. https://investedwallet.com/investing-terms-for-beginners/

Lessons from Warren Buffett's Gift for Language and Storytelling. (2018, February 7). https://www.ishmaelscorner.com/storytelling-lessons-from-warren-buffetts/

Lincoln, T. M. (2019, October 18). 18 Stock Market Investing Myths and the Facts That Debunk Them. https://medium.com/better-marketing/18-stock-market-investing-myths-and-the-facts-that-debunk-them-df42d9de8c5d

MacKay, J. (2020, February 6). Warren Buffett Increased His Wealth 7,268% Using This 1 Method. https://www.inc.com/jory-mackay/1-simple-technique-made-warren-buffett-billions-he.html

Miller, J. C. (2016, May 16). This Warren Buffett rule can work wonders on your portfolio. https://www.marketwatch.com/story/this-warren-buffett-rule-can-work-wonders-on-your-portfolio-2016-04-26

moneychimp.com. (2020b). Compound Interest Calculator. http://www.moneychimp.com/calculator/compound_interest_calculator.htm

Montag, A. (2019, January 2). Billionaire Ray Dalio shares a 3-step formula for anyone to start investing. https://www.cnbc.com/2019/01/02/ray-dalio-shares-formula-anyone-can-use-to-start-investing.html

O'Shea, A. (2020, June 8). How to Invest in Stocks. https://www.nerdwallet.com/article/investing/how-to-invest-in-stocks

Proctor, C. (2020, April 3). What is dollar-cost averaging? A simple investment strategy that will help most people build wealth over time. https://www.businessinsider.com/personal-finance/what-is-dollar-cost-averaging-a-way-to-build-wealth-over-time?international=true&r=US&IR=T

Reinkensmeyer, B. (2020, June 10). Best Online Brokers 2020. https://www.stockbrokers.com/guides/online-stock-brokers

ROBBINS RESEARCH INTERNATIONAL, INC. (2019, June 4). 12 Financial Terms & Business Terms You Should Know | Tony Robbins. https://www.tonyrobbins.com/wealth-lifestyle/12-financial-terms-need-know/

ROBBINS RESEARCH INTERNATIONAL, INC. (2020, February 11). Compound Interest: Definition, How it Works & More. https://www.tonyrobbins.com/ask-tony/power-of-compounding/

Serwer, A. (2019, April 29). Warren Buffett explains how you could've turned $114 into $400,000 with a simple long-term investment. https://sg.finance.yahoo.com/news/warren-buffett-says-couldve-turned-114-400000-230140222.html

Staff, M. (2019, October 9). Stock Trading Terms - Stock Terms Every Investor Needs to Know. https://www.marketbeat.com/financial-terms/

Templeton, J. (2017). 10 Principles for Investment Success. https://www.franklintempleton.lu/content-international/pdf/FTIFLU_MAXIMS_0217.pdf

Tuchman, M. (2017, June 6). 7 timeless investing lessons from Vanguard founder John Bogle. https://www.marketwatch.com/story/7-timeless-investing-lessons-from-vanguard-founder-john-bogle-2017-06-06

Tweddale, A. (2019, April 29). If You Still Don't Believe in the Power of Compound Interest, You Have to See This. https://www.moneyunder30.com/power-of-compound-interest

Whitt, L. (2019, April 9). Isabel Cabrera. https://addicted2success.com/success-advice/5-key-investment-principles-from-warren-buffett/

Wikipedia contributors. (2020, June 13). Mr. Market. https://en.wikipedia.org/wiki/Mr._Market

Yeo, J. (2017, August 8). Warren Buffett: The Difference between Investing, Speculating and Gambling. https://www.smallcapasia.com/warren-buffett-difference-between-investing-and-gambling/

www.ingramcontent.com/pod-product-compliance
Lightning Source LLC
LaVergne TN
LVHW011816200926
848484LV00005B/1216